A TRUE STORY OF OVERCOMING
SEEMINGLY IMPOSSIBLE ODDS

# THE
# BRAVEST GUY

HARRY E. WEDEWER

*The Bravest Guy*
Copyright © 2016 by Harry E. Wedewer. All rights reserved.
First Print Edition: October 2016

ISBN-13: 978-1539098874
ISBN-10: 1539098877

Library of Congress Control Number: 2016916142
CreateSpace Independent Publishing Platform, North Charleston, SC

For more about this work visit www.bravestguy.com
To contact the author email: harry@wedewergroup.com
Cover and Formatting: Streetlight Graphics

To my mother and father.

To the love of my life, Robin, and my son, Ben, and to my sister, and all of my brothers and their families.

And to those who have served, and who continue to serve in the defense of this great nation.

The United States of America, and to their families.

I am merely a scribe who has told another's story.

*When one door of happiness closes, another opens;
but often we look so long at the closed door that we do
not see the one which has been opened for us.*

*– Helen Keller – We Bereaved, 1929*

# PROLOGUE

More than 70 years have passed since a day that was, and remains for me, unimaginable. My father, Don Wedewer, was nearly dead. In fact, he should have been dead.

Then a 19-year-old Army infantry private, he lay badly wounded in slushy snow, fading in and out of consciousness, his face bleeding from the blast that moments before had shattered the hospital in Liège, Belgium, where he was a patient. It was November 24, 1944, the day after Thanksgiving, and almost three years since the United States had entered World War II. The hospital had been shredded by a German V-1 "Buzz Bomb." The Vergeltungswaffe 1 — Revenge Weapon No. 1, as it was called by the Germans — was an indiscriminate terror weapon, a long-range flying bomb loaded with almost 2,000 pounds of high explosives. It was a cross between a SCUD missile of First Gulf War infamy and a flying improvised explosive device (IED) of more recent notoriety in the wars in Iraq and Afghanistan. Like later weapons, the V-1 was crude but gruesomely effective, exacting revenge by indiscriminately destroying and killing everything and everyone in its path.

Two days earlier in Liège, in a particularly horrific bombing, a careening V-1 had ricocheted off the top of a street trolley and crashing into the second floor of a girls' school before exploding, killing dozens and injuring many more. One historian described the V-1 as the World War II equivalent of the cinematic *Terminator*: "It can't be reasoned with; it doesn't feel pity or remorse or fear. It absolutely will not stop."[1] In short, nothing was sacred or secure from the V-1. And in Liège, there was virtually no defense against it.

Sometimes you had warning it was coming. On the horizon, the V-1 first appeared as a speck. As it drew closer it looked like a black cross[2] streaking across the sky while emitting a guttural roar. It was an unnerving sound, similar to that made by a pack of Harley-Davidson motorcycles. The roar abruptly stopped with a distinctive *"click"* as the V-1's motor cut off. Then followed 14 seconds of terrifying silence as it plunged to earth to annihilate whatever lay in its path. In describing the psychological effect of the terror bombing of Liège by the V-1s, one soldier wrote: "Mere words are highly inadequate to portray the terror and noise and death which all occur at the height of battle or bombing."[3]

It was shortly after nine o'clock in the morning.[4] The ground around the two-story brick buildings of the hospital was wet with slushy snow. Dad had just been moved to a recovery room after being x-rayed. His body — or what was left of it — was in a full body cast. His tissue was perforated by shrapnel, one eye was gone, his teeth were blown in, and one finger had the knuckle blown off. Worst of all, both legs were severed, one above the knee, the other below the knee. Four days before, while in combat in Germany, Private First Class Wedewer had stepped on a land mine.

Dad had heard plenty of V-1s while in the combat zone. That morning, though, he didn't hear it coming. No sirens, no calls to take cover. No warning at all. One moment he was lying immobilized in the serenity of the recovery room; the next, the blast from the bomb's impact catapulted him into the air and then slammed him back onto the bed. The ceiling collapsed on top of him. A rafter came crashing down and landed across his chest, pinning him to the bed. Pieces of the ceiling, now a barrage of razor-like projectiles, slashed his face.

The blast concussed my father, causing the retina in his one good eye to detach, leaving him nearly blind. Almost everyone in the nearby x-ray room, from where he'd just been moved, was dead. By one account, the blast was so powerful that bodies were tossed up to 75 feet and were left hanging over the ceiling rafters, where some died before they could be rescued.⁵ A courageous nurse, seeing my father's helplessness, fetched help to get him out and laid him in the wet snow outside. Around him were wreckage, fire, and many dead, both civilians and soldiers. Sightless and fading in and out of consciousness, my father heard a Catholic priest giving him the Catholic sacrament of Last Rights in French. In the Catholic faith, this is a final blessing given to someone expected to die: *"Par cette onction sainte, que le Seigneur, en sa grande bonté, vous réconforte par la grâce de l'Esprit Saint ...* (Through this holy anointing may the Lord in his love and mercy help you with the grace of the Holy Spirit) ... *Ainsi, vous ayant libéré de tous péchés, qu'il vous sauve et vous relève ...* (May the Lord who frees you from sin save you and raise you up ...)."

Having grown up in a small town in Iowa, my father didn't know any French. However, even in his semi-conscious state, he knew what was going on: he was being given-up for dead. Again.

This was the *second* time my father had received Last Rights in less than a week. Four days earlier, advancing on an enemy fortification in the Hürtgen Forest on the western edge of Germany, he'd been given up for dead when his legs were blown off after stepping on a mine. On that occasion too, a priest had stood over him and uttered the same blessing. Subsequently, Dad had been moved to the hospital in Liège, a "safe" area miles from the fighting where wounded soldiers could be further stabilized. Now, in this supposedly safe area, Dad sustained injuries which were as bad, or perhaps worse, than those he had suffered in combat days earlier.

Thousands of miles away, in the small town of Dyersville in the Midwestern cornfields of Iowa, the Reverend John B. Herbers, an ordinarily stern, bespectacled parish priest at St. Francis Xavier Church, broke down in tears as he told his congregation that Private First Class Don Wedewer was wounded. Don Wedewer, the gangly, boyish-looking hometown kid; the altar boy, baseball player, student at St. Francis Xavier School next door, and someone who Reverend Herbers wanted to be a priest, instead went off to war. Now, he would never be the same.

At about the same time, a local newspaper reported: "*Dyersville Infantryman Is Wounded on German Front*"[6] and published a photo of my father in uniform, looking every bit as young as his 19 years. The newspaper article did not disclose the nature of my father's wounds, but noted that a nurse wrote the letter home informing his family that he was wounded. This was not a good sign.

These scenes could have played out many times in a war that killed more than 405,000[7] Americans and wounded more than 670,000[8] others. Among those were eight from Dyersville who did not make it back from the war: Staff Sergeant Clarence Ries, killed in action; Private First Class John Rahe, killed in action; Technical Sergeant, Cyril Christoph, killed in action;[9] and there were others.[10] What Reverend Herbers and the newspaper probably didn't know, though, was how close to death PFC Wedewer came. By a razor-thin margin, he was among those who would make it home.

My father's wounds, however, would not be the hardest thing to deal with on his journey back.

---

Decades later, as I read about maimed young veterans returning from the wars in Afghanistan and Iraq, I think of my father and his long path to recovery. At the same time, I realize that his story is not about one war and its aftermath. Rather, his is a story that transcends all wars.

One haunting image strikes me in particular. An Army Private First Class shot in the stomach in Afghanistan clutches a rosary as he is medically evacuated. Different war, different context, and decades later. Yet, in that image and others like it, I see my father.

After researching my father's story, I can only begin to comprehend the challenges faced by veterans wounded in recent wars. What I do know, though, if my father's experience is any guide, is that the challenges are daunting. There will be doubt. There will be setbacks. And there may be resentment as to "Why me?" My father faced these challenges on a journey that led to his becoming the director of a state agency in Florida, a presidential appointee, and a member of the Blind Hall of Fame; a journey that led to recognition from four U.S. presidents—all while my mother, Marabeth, raised my three brothers, my sister, and me.

Like many of the World War II generation, my father rarely talked about the war. Even now, he instinctively resists doing so out of concern that he would sound as if he were grandstanding. My father hates that.

He is not someone I have known well. But in retracing his steps through the suffering of terrible wounds and recovery, I came to know him—and myself—better. Why sons seek to know their fathers better is something I cannot explain. It is something I simply felt compelled to do.

This book, though, is not about me. It is about my father. Retracing his unlikely steps around the country and overseas was a more protracted process than I anticipated.

In over a decade, drawing inspiration from, among others, the great contemporary historians David McCullough, Doris Kearns Goodwin, and Douglas Brinkley, I had to touch and feel history where it happened. My travels and perspective on the following pages are significant only to the extent that they somehow illuminate my father's past.

Ultimately, I hope a brief telling of his story will help others. I know it has been an inspiration to me.

# 1
# BEGINNINGS

ACCORDING TO FAMILY LORE, MY father's grandfather, Bernard Heinrich ("Barney") Wedewer, hated war. In 1866, after fighting as a young man in the Seven-Weeks War in his native Germany, where he was a part of the killing, maiming, and destruction, Barney had had enough. In the late 1860s, Barney, along with his brothers, left Germany.

After reaching America, he eventually journeyed to eastern Iowa and settled near the town of Dyersville to farm. It was life far removed from the increasing militarism in Germany. My father always said the Germans were "land crazy" — that accumulating land was a life's mission. For Grandfather Wedewer, eastern Iowa with its vast tracts of fertile land must have seemed like the end of the rainbow.

This part of Iowa is gently rolling terrain with patches of trees in otherwise endless fields of corn dotted by ubiquitous farm silos. Reflecting the area's German influence, families with names such as Klostermann, Deutmeyer, Becker, and Werner established farms on the fertile land around Dyersville.[11] It was here that Barney Wedewer settled down to farm and eventually married into one of the area's landholding families, the Paskers.

Barney Wedewer never lost his hatred of war. At one point, he ran off his property someone who came around to sell bonds to support the Spanish-American War.

---

Dyersville was and still is classic small-town America. A farming hub founded by English settlers in the mid 19th century, the town serves as a market and transportation center for the surrounding farms. In 1941, when the United States entered World War II, the population numbered only about 2,000. In those days, Dyersville was bisected by Highway 20, which ran east to west south of town, and the tracks of the Illinois Central Railroad, which ran parallel to the highway on the north side of town. These arteries connected Dyersville with the larger city of Dubuque and the Mississippi River, about a two-hour drive to the east.

Dyersville's main thoroughfare is lined with businesses that serve the farming community, and Victorian-style homes, some dating back to the town's beginning. In my father's childhood during the 1920s and '30s, the business district was also dotted with beer gardens, reflecting the area's strong German ties, where farmers relaxed after a long day in the fields.

More recently, Dyersville found fame as the site of the "Field of Dreams" in the well-known baseball movie.[12] Every year, tens of thousands of people, some from as far away as Japan and Australia, visit a baseball field on the edge of town cut out of corn stalks. In the movie, ghostly images of baseball players return here to relive their past glories. The attraction of this rather ordinary field to the approximately 80,000 visitors who come annually might seem odd to some, but ask the devoted baseball fans among the visitors to the Field of Dreams and you will likely get a different response. This is Dyersville, a place where what might seem quaint and ordinary — perhaps even stifling — to some, takes on the magic of a contented life with a refreshing simplicity and clarity.

The other dominant influence in town, aside from farming, is the old basilica or "Pope's Church" of St. Francis Xavier. Built in the 1880s, St. Francis Xavier, which can seat approximately 1,200 parishioners, is an imposing presence in Dyersville.[13] Its twin spires reach 212 feet high and are capped by 14-foot-high gold leaf crosses that can be seen for miles. Viewed from afar through cornfields on the edge of town, St. Francis Xavier's soaring spires give visitors the uncanny impression of a mirage-like Wizard of Oz Emerald City. Financing to build the church came from twelve local families who mortgaged their farms, thus risking their futures. That act was emblematic of the inseparable compact between the

Church and the community, and the latter's compulsion to make a dramatically visual statement of their faith. With its imposing size and Gothic architecture, St. Francis Xavier is the sort of church you would expect to find in a historic European town or some older, upscale neighborhood in the United States, but not in a rural farming community in the Midwest.

The interior of St. Francis Xavier is equally impressive. Its 64 stained-glass windows form a backdrop that showers its soaring columns and vaulted ceilings with kaleidoscopic streams of color and soft light. The centerpiece of this panorama is a painting on the ceiling above the main altar depicting in vivid colors a radiant Lamb of God surrounded by angels. The scene purposefully gives worshipers a sense of peering into heaven. It is the sort of church where, even if you pay no attention to what's being said, the visuals alone create lasting, interwoven impressions of the power and authority of virtue.

One of those on whom St. Francis Xavier created a lasting impression was my father, Don Wedewer. He grew up attending church services there every school day while he was a pupil at St. Francis Xavier School next door. Underscoring the visuals of the church, the services in those days were in Latin. This gave the Mass ritual even more of an air of sanctity and certitude in the faith along with its mystery. Here was a place where one could reflexively find refuge in hours of need through such prayers as the Act of Contrition. No doubt, his memories of St. Francis Xavier served as a spiritual refuge for my father in his later hours of need.

———

Dad's father (my grandfather), Bernard "Ben" Wedewer, started out making a living on the land, in the tradition of his own father, Barney, In Ben's case this was by driving a steam-powered corn thresher — a hulking piece of farm equipment designed to remove the corn kernels from the cornstalk in bulk. With his thresher, Ben was a journeyman of sorts who rented his threshing services out to area farmers.

Like his father, Ben married into a local landholding family, who owned a farm southwest of town. Ben's 1915 wedding picture, in which he is seated next to his bride, Josephine Schlarmann, seems to characterize the man. He is ramrod straight and handsome with his black hair slicked back. He has a focused, confident look that gives him the appearance of a corporate chief executive officer, coach, or military commander who has few moments of self-doubt. Indeed, that was Ben.

Although Ben started out making his living off the land, he eventually left it and became a builder. Over time, he ventured into other businesses.

Like his father, Ben was bilingual, speaking both English and German. He had a habit of breaking into German when haggling over a price with his customers.

As was the case with many families in Dyersville, German influence permeated the Wedewer household: sauerkraut, beer, Catholic upbringing, and the family name. To this day, though, perhaps like other veterans of World War II, my father loathes all things German.

My father was the second-youngest of his parents' six boys. Josephine, his mother, died in 1937 when he was 11, and his father remarried. As Dad remembers it, Ben Wedewer's second wife, Agatha Pins Trenkamp, was more of a caretaker who, aside from keeping up the house, was mostly disengaged from her stepsons. She went about her business and my father and his brothers went about theirs. Perhaps this lack of a strong maternal influence was the reason my father and his brothers were not particularly close. However, one characteristic they did share was a kind of stubbornness. It was a hard-headedness that meant that a Wedewer could not be dislodged from his certainty on a particular issue or goal he held. Once a Wedewer became entrenched, he would not budge. As disagreeable as this trait might seem, if channeled in the right direction, such stubbornness could manifest itself as uncommon persistence, a simple refusal to give up. During some bleak days to come, my father would discover that such unwavering persistence would become a life-saving gift.

As for Ben Wedewer, by the time my father was growing up, he had become a big man, both literally and figuratively. Before he lost some of his business enterprise in the economic Great Depression of the early 1930s, Ben was the richest person in Dyersville. Aside from being a general contractor, he owned Grant Highway Park, which was the nearest thing in Dyersville to an amusement park.

This entertainment complex included a tavern that prominently announced it had "tables for ladies," as well as a dance hall, roller rink, and an exposition center for public events including boxing matches.[14] Grant Highway Park also hosted pole sitting. This was a rather odd form of public entertainment in which people would bet on how long someone could sit atop a high pole at the park. A guy named Bill Penfield sat on the pole for 79 days and even stood up during his fifth week to show he wasn't paralyzed.[15] However, Penfield was bested by Andy Robinson who sat atop the pole for 87 days.[16] Pole sitting had all the suspense of betting on how long it would take grass to grow. Such was life in 1930s Dyersville.

---

A Wedewer to the core, Ben was opinionated. He didn't have much use for President Franklin Roosevelt and his progressive, "big government" policies. This was particularly the case after passage of the National Recovery Act, which limited the number of hours that businesses such as Ben's could work their employees. The theory was, the fewer hours employees could work, the more would need to be hired.

Ben Wedewer also drank too much. At a young age, Dad would find his father's empty liquor bottles in the family's garage. He also remembered his father's slurred speech. Perhaps it was his father's drinking, the death of his mother at an early age, his detached stepmother — or perhaps some other circumstance — that developed my father's ability to cope with what happened to him. This coping skill he later combined with an unfaltering sense of optimism.

Whether it came from his mother, or was a reflexive rejection of his father's loud, opinionated demeanor, Dad also had an innate resistance to braggarts and those he perceived as bullies.

Whatever Ben Wedewer's flaws, though, my father inherited his ability to build things, if not literally then figuratively, and the related ability to act on his vision, unafraid of the risks.

Ben Wedewer also provided for his six sons during the economic calamity of the Great Depression. By Depression-era standards, the Wedewers were relatively fortunate. At a time when one in four Americans was without a job and breadlines were common, the family had a house and food. And, somehow, Ben Wedewer's businesses more or less survived.

As a result, while growing up, my father had the opportunity to do what boys generally did in Dyersville — play baseball, swim in the local river, hang out at the local filling station, or gas station, which was a man's place, and attend Catholic school. Going to Catholic school meant being taught by rather taciturn nuns and attending Mass every day, along with a heavy dose of religious education and liberally dispensed corporal punishment. This was all complemented by Reverend Herbers' fire-and-brimstone preaching at daily and Sunday Mass.

To be sure, such education was not free of its moral ambiguities. There was Charlie Gephardt, Dad's baseball coach, who tended to play things on the edge. For example, he would hide baseballs in the outfield to cheat opposing teams, and when he took the young players to Chicago to see a White Sox baseball game, they would sneak through the back door of a drugstore to avoid paying the fare for the train.

However, Charlie was the exception. Whatever its merits, or some might say demerits, his Catholic education imbued my father with a strong moral compass that even the Charlies of the world could not confound. At bottom, he was a good kid.

Although life in pre-World War II Dyersville may have appeared monochromatic — when it seemed everyone had a German-sounding last name, everyone had something to do with farming, and everyone was Catholic — such a relative cocoon insulated one from inherited biases and attendant baggage of being uncomfortable around others because they were different. In Dyersville, there was generally no preconceived *us* against *them*.

My father's simple upbringing in Dyersville nurtured his character. That, combined with his ingrained sense of optimism and ability to accept things as they were, would equip him well for what lay ahead.

# 2
# THE WAR

THE GREEK HISTORIAN HERODOTUS WROTE, "No one is so foolish as to prefer war to peace, in which, instead of sons burying their fathers, fathers bury their sons."[17] Such was the case in Dyersville. As idyllic as life there may have been, the town could not escape the impact of national and international events. During the Civil War, four young men from Dyersville were killed in action.[18] During World War I, 11 young men left for the war and did not return.[19] Now, in 1941, war again intruded on Dyersville's doorstep like an unwelcome guest, to stake its claim on the town's most valuable asset—its young men and women.

While my father was growing up in the 1930s, there was awareness in Dyersville of the increasing danger posed by the rise of fascism abroad. It was a faint but nonetheless troubling storm. In Europe, Adolph Hitler, and the reign of terror inspired by his fascist Nazism spread across Germany and then continental Europe as a whole. In January 1939, Hitler warned that war would bring about "the annihilation of the Jewish race in Europe."[20] With the outbreak of war that September, against England, France, and their allies, he and his henchmen proceeded to carry out this threat. Through mobile "gas vans," dedicated "killing centers," and concentration camps, the Nazis murdered Jews, Gypsies, and any other people the Nazis deemed "unfit."[21] Describing the Nazis' subsequent invasion of Russia, British Prime Minister Winston Churchill lamented, "Since the Mongol invasions of Europe in the Sixteenth century, there has never been methodical, merciless butchery on such a scale, or approaching such a scale ... We are in the presence of a crime without a name."[22]

In Asia, Japan sought to subjugate large portions of China

and other parts of Asia under the guise of a "Greater East Asia Co-Prosperity Sphere that would ensure "Asia for Asiatics."[23] The Japanese message to America was blunt: stay out. In a shockingly brutal episode in 1937, Imperial Japanese Army forces slaughtered hundreds of thousands of civilians in the Chinese city of Nanking, and sexually assaulted tens of thousands of women in what became infamously known as the "Rape of Nanking."[24]

Waves of destruction, terror, and killing, fueled by ethnic and religious hatred continued to spread like metastasizing cancerous growths that blotted out national borders and any semblance of independent thought, much less freedom. It is not an overstatement to say that democracy, if not civil society as we knew it, was at a point of inflection, and in danger of slipping into an abyss. Americans began to realize collectively that, as imperfect as many democracies may have been at the time, free societies were systematically being extinguished around the world.

In recognition of the rapidly deteriorating situation overseas, on May 27, 1941, President Franklin Roosevelt declared a state of "unlimited national emergency" after warning the nation that the war was "coming very close to home."[25] Roosevelt presented the threat and the response as a stark one: "We will not accept a Hitler-dominated world ... We will accept only a world consecrated to freedom of speech and expression—freedom of every person to worship God in his own way—freedom from want—and freedom from terror."[26]

The existential nature of the threat, however, was not a feeling universally held in a country with a strong isolationist streak. This sentiment was a leftover from the belief by many in the United States that it had needlessly entered World War I. This in turn engendered skepticism over whether a war-weary country should become embroiled in another overseas conflict. Yet, as the country rapidly rebuilt its armed forces after years of neglect, the situation only worsened.

During my father's youth, the events in Europe and Asia, and the possibility of war, were frequent topics of conversation at the filling station and barbershop. Even before the advent of the 24-hour news cycle there was uneasiness that events overseas in unrecognizable places, involving people with unrecognizable names, could spiral out of control and come crashing back home. As was the case with Americans who remember where they were when they learned of the terrorist attacks on September 11, 2001, it is no exaggeration to say that everyone in my father's generation remembers where they were when they heard the news of the Japanese attack on Pearl Harbor on December 7, 1941.

In that single morning at Pearl Harbor, 2,390 Americans were killed and another 1,178 wounded.[27] The grainy video of the battleship USS *Arizona* exploding in a fireball, killing 1,177 sailors and marines in a flash,[28] was horrifically similar in scope to that of the twin towers crashing down in New York City almost 60 years later. As with 9/11, American reaction to the Pearl Harbor attack was a mixture of shock, horror, and outrage. The Japanese admiral who conceived the Pearl Harbor attack is said to have prophetically stated: "I fear that all we have done is to wake a sleeping giant and fill him with a terrible resolve."[29] Similarly, infuriated by the destruction at Pearl Harbor, a U.S. Navy Admiral, William Halsey, stated: "Before we're through with 'em, the Japanese language will be spoken only in hell!"[30] Indeed, for Americans after Pearl Harbor, it was all-in, total war against Japan and its Axis German and Italian allies in Europe.

As was true of many of his generation, my father's entry into the Army grew from an unwavering desire to serve. It was never a question of *if*, only *how*. By war's end, all five of his brothers were in government service. Dad's armed forces draft notice arrived in July 1943, barely a month after he graduated from high school and only a few days after his 18th birthday. The notice ordered him to report to Camp Dodge, in Johnston, Iowa, for processing into the armed forces. Had the notice not arrived, he would have joined anyway. Offered a temporary draft deferment due to working in his father's business, Dad refused. Encouraged by his parish priest, Reverend Herbers, to enter the priesthood and thus avoid immediate military service, the answer from my father: "Nope." Offered a chance to sign up with the Army Air Corps or the Navy during his draft induction, my father's response, again, was a polite no. Seemingly, nothing was going to stop Dad from fulfilling his destiny in the United States Army.

---

To my father's seeming good fortune, he scored high enough on placement exams to enter the Army Specialized Training Program, or ASTP, through which he would attend college and receive an officer's commission. Before doing so, however, he would have to endure the rigors of approximately 17 weeks of Army basic training. First stop, then, in October 1943, was the Army Infantry Replacement Training Center at Camp Wolters, Texas. The camp was in Mineral Wells, west of Fort Worth in a mostly flat, rather barren part of Texas.

Camp Wolters was a sprawling reservation covering approximately 16,000 acres.[31] It later served as a helicopter training center through the Vietnam War, and is now an industrial park. Today, a historic marker at the site notes that approximately 30,000 soldiers went through the camp in a single training cycle during World War II, a minute reminder of the vastness of the war effort. Overall, the place was enormous. Camp Wolters encompassed six different housing areas for the soldier trainees with seemingly endless rows of white two-story barracks arrayed in perfectly straight columns. As one of the cogs in this vast training machine, PFC Donald H. Wedewer, Serial Number 37679214, Infantry Replacement Training Unit, Company B, 63rd Battalion, 14th Regiment, drew pay of $50.00 per month.[32]

Along with other ASTPers who arrived at Camp Wolters in late 1943, my father learned that the ASTP program was being closed down—in Dad's case by reading about it in a newspaper. Eighteen-year-olds such as PFC Wedewer were not needed as officers after all. Instead, they were required as foot soldiers or infantryman on the front lines of combat. They would fill the need for replacement soldiers to support the ground offensives in Europe, and for the anticipated invasion of Japan. The calculation was simple: more of our young people were needed on the front lines to kill more of their young people. So in one swoop, the Army took approximately 100,000 officer candidates — a stunning number — including many who were already enrolled in college or, like Dad, were in Infantry Replacement Training Units, and plugged some of them into deployed units whose ranks were decimated by combat losses. Other infantry replacements were sent to round out units preparing to deploy overseas. Aside from being a rather unglamorous designation, "infantry replacement" was also a dangerous one. It could mean that you were being fast-tracked into a unit that, in all likelihood, would see combat sooner rather than later.[33]

Dad accepted the news with characteristic stoicism, perhaps not thinking of what this could mean for his future. In any case, he probably had little time to dwell on it. My father's basic training, like that of millions of soldiers before and after, was designed to shock the system and mold the human gamut of all sizes and shapes into a stereotypical soldier, capable of killing on behalf of their country. The Army guide at the time expressed this ethos:

> "I am training to be an infantryman. I am proud, for I know that when the last enemy stronghold is captured, it will be an infantryman, supported on the ground and in the air by thousands of other men, who will have captured that stronghold and held it. As an infantryman, I must be a many-skilled soldier, more than a rifleman, a machine gunner, or a cannoneer. I must learn all that is necessary to achieve success in battle, to defeat and capture or destroy the enemy ... Because I am fighting to live, I must keep myself informed of the progress

of my fight. I must know why I fight, and follow and appreciate the progress of millions of my fellows and millions of my allies as they help me in this fight across seven seas and seven continents. As soon as I have learned to take care of myself, I must learn how to take care of what Uncle Sam has given me. I must know how to care for my clothes and equipment. Waste means delay in my study to become a soldier. After I have learned how to live, I must learn how to fight."[34]

A consequence of Great Depression-era economics was that significant numbers of the 18-year-olds who arrived at Camp Wolters and similar camps to learn how to fight, grew up in impoverished circumstances and thus reported for duty malnourished. In part, this led to today's federally funded school lunch and breakfast programs. How to turn this diverse mass of half-starved army draftees into trained soldiers to kill Germans and Japanese presented an enormous challenge.

What *didn't* pose a challenge were any lingering moral dilemmas that PFC Wedewer and his fellow trainees may have had about killing the Germans or Japanese. There were largely none. In today's context, it was if ISIS or Al Qaeda and their acolytes had seized large parts of the world. Thus, little thought was given to the ethics of killing Germans or Japanese. This view was reflected in the pop culture of the day, in songs such as, "We're Going to Stop That Dirty Little Jap" and "We've Got to Do a Job on the Japs Baby,"[35] which were used to stoke ethnic and racial enmity among the American public. As Army General George Patton observed at the time, "May God have mercy for my enemies because I won't."[36]

The killer instinct that the Army attempted to instill in young trainees such as Dad is captured perfectly in the 1943 Army training film *Kill or Be Killed*.[37] From the outset, in rapid-fire, sneering delivery, the narrator sternly intones over American sports film clips that the spirit of America is "fast and hard-hitting and clean." But, he continues, "When you step from the [football] gridiron to the no man's land of the battlefield, the rule book is buried and forgotten ... War is the law of the jungle. It is kill or be killed! You have got to twist your instincts inside out to play this game ... The goal is destruction, plain and simple. To hurt, to cripple, to kill. This is war!"

The hurt, cripple or kill part is stressed just as the film cuts to a soldier kneeing a bad guy in his genitals, perhaps in an attempt to appeal to the 18-year-old-male sense of humor. In around nine minutes, the film depicts close to two dozen ways to hurt or kill the enemy. You can shoot him with an array of weapons: tommy gun, rifle, carbine, machine gun, Browning Automatic Rifle (BAR), pistol, or even the heretofore illegal sawed off shot gun ("pride of the underworld, reinstated for the duration"); you can blow him up using a hand grenade, mortar, or cannon; or you can kill the bad guy using more basic means, ranging from the especially brutal (knife to just about every part of the body, or smashing him in the head or face with all kinds of stuff) to the less bloody (kicking him in the genitals shows up again) to the almost comedic (stomp on his foot—albeit a hard stomp).

Gallows humor runs throughout *Kill or be Killed*, for example, the advice to toss a grenade in the dugout where the enemy is hiding and "let 'em divide it," or a lesson on "how to lift a Nazi's face without improving his looks." Not a word in *Kill or be Killed* addresses the rules of engagement, laws of war, or winning hearts and minds so prominent in modern wars. Apparently, the Germans and Japanese not only didn't merit respect, they didn't deserve mercy, either. Turning the enemy into a sub-human object was key to developing the killer mentality.

With this sort of motivation, as campy and propaganda-laden as my father thought it was, he and his fellow trainees were trained to shoot an array of weapons the names of which he could still rattle off more than six decades later. There was the M-1 rifle (his favorite), the smaller M-1 carbine, the Browning Automatic Rifle, the 30-caliber machine gun, the 53-millimeter mortar, the

81-millimeter mortar, the bazooka (a rocket-propelled grenade), and more. It was an incredible arsenal placed in the hands of teenagers. For many, the only violence they had seen was in Hollywood westerns and gangster films. Before leaving home, they could never have imagined that, one day, they would be real-life soldiers.

Every day at Camp Wolters was scripted pretty much the same:

| | |
|---|---|
| 6:00 a.m. | Reveille (some guy blowing a bugle) |
| 6:45 a.m. | Breakfast (or "chow," as the Army called the menu of universally grey foods) |
| 7:00 a.m. | Clean-up |
| 7:30–12:00 noon | Instruction (learning to shoot and blow things up) |
| 12:00–1:00 p.m. | Chow (more grey food) |
| 1:00–4:30 p.m. | More Instruction (more shooting and blowing things up) |
| 5:15 p.m. | Retreat |
| 5:30 p.m. | Chow (yes, more grey food) |
| Free time | |
| 11:00 p.m. | Taps (the guy blowing the bugle again).[38] |

During the "Instruction" period, Dad and the trainees spent day after day in the field. These field exercises included crawling under barbed wire with machine guns firing over their heads and explosions being set off around them, riding on the backs of tanks, and crouching in dugouts as tanks literally ran over their heads — the latter intended to reduce the young recruits' fear of the ominous-looking tanks. On one such occasion, one of my father's buddies became a little over-zealous and started firing his Browning Automatic Rifle at a tank, Hollywood shoot 'em-up style, much to the discomfort of the tankers, who constantly stressed that there were slits to the open air on the tanks.

Period photos taken at Camp Wolters generally depict the

instructors striking the same pose: ramrod straight, hands on their hips, feet spread apart in a stance that says, "I can't fucking believe that we are making fucking soldiers out of these fucking guys." But, soldiers they were to become.

Indeed, my father seemed to thrive on being a soldier during basic training, as improbable as that may have seemed for a skinny, six foot two inch, not particularly aggressive former altar boy from small-town Iowa. But Dad had all of the characteristics of a dutiful, good soldier. For example, he was particularly proud of his skills with his rifle—the M-1 Garand. The M-1 was a semi-automatic, wooden-stock rifle with a short barrel protruding from the end. Semi-automatic meant that a soldier didn't have to eject the empty bullet shell from the rifle after each shot. With the M-1, the soldier dropped an eight-cartridge clip into the receiver on the top of the rifle. Once seated, a round would be pushed from the clip into the rifle chamber. After each bullet was fired, the empty bullet casing was automatically ejected from the weapon, and a new round was chambered until the clip was empty, at which point it too was ejected. For its day, the M-1 was considered an advanced weapon and was popular with soldiers for its robustness and reliability.[39]

His proficiency with the M-1 and mastery of the other infantryman skills later earned my father the Expert Infantryman Badge—a considerable achievement. The badge meant he was expert with several weapons, had completed rigorous physical fitness tests and lengthy marches in full combat gear, and had successfully completed combat simulation courses.[40] More than seven decades later, he was as proud of that badge as anything he accomplished before or since.

---

Aside from introducing my father to the basics of Army life, Camp Wolters left him with some other lasting impressions. One was the poor treatment of African-American soldiers, who were segregated into separate units under the armed services' policy of that era. On the way to training exercises, he recalled passing the dilapidated barracks where African-American soldiers were housed. This was characteristic of their separate and unequal treatment. It was the first time my father had seen segregation, and in this case it even extended to the service clubs—there were clubs for white soldiers and clubs for African-American soldiers. Nor was it any different for African-American soldiers off base. If they stepped on a train or a bus, or went into a restaurant, theater, or soda fountain, or even went to the bathroom or took a sip of water from a drinking fountain, they had to heed the signs: "Colored Only." No matter how much of an outrage it might seem today, such mistreatment was the norm in World War II society.[41]

My father's other lasting image of Mineral Wells was the Baker Hotel. This was a rather ornate, high-rise structure, left over from the city's bygone days as a resort. By the year 2000, when I visited Mineral Wells, the Baker Hotel was shuttered and ramshackle. As I walked the path between the front gate of Camp Wolters and the hotel, as my father would have done, the Baker seemed a distant mirage, out of place amid the drabness of Camp Wolters and its environs. In its heyday, dinner at the Baker probably seemed like heaven to my father.

On his return from dinner at the Baker, or from other off-base journeys, my father and other soldiers were subjected to the ignominious "short-arm" inspection. Essentially, this meant lining up in the middle of the night in front of a doctor while wearing only a raincoat. One by one, the doctors would check the soldier's private parts for any indication of venereal disease. Such cases were apparently not unheard of in Mineral Wells, because it earned the unfortunate nickname of "Venereal Wells" among some soldiers. To discourage activity that led to venereal disease, the trainees were subjected to numerous "training films" featuring alluring women who warned of the hazards of consorting with the opposite sex. In retrospect, such images seem a bit counterintuitive, particularly for an installation that was likely full of sex-starved 18 – and 19-year-olds. For a Catholic teenager from Iowa, it was a rather maturing experience.

During my visit to the former Camp Wolters, I also encountered the proud manager of the Camp Wolters motor pool, whose singular mission was to restore old Army vehicles. I had the sense that no one ever inquired about his fleet of vintage trucks, and he was eager to show them off. Because of my interest, I was treated to a tour of the base in an authentically restored 1941 Army truck. I told my host that I was there to learn more about my father. I also told him that my father thought I was crazy to travel all that way to visit a decrepit former Army base — a place in a barren part of Texas that even the locals seemingly had given up on. My otherwise polite host cut me off mid sentence. He understood. *I had to be there.*

During my impromptu tour of the former camp, we stopped at some of the remaining World War II barracks of the kind my father stayed in — abandoned for decades after the base closed and had become a patchwork industrial site. The barracks were rectangular, two-story, 55-person, wooden structures with sloped metal roofs, and long open bays accommodating bedding on either side. A wood-burning stove stood in the middle. On the bottom floor at one end were group bathroom and shower facilities with open pipes. It was utilitarian to be sure, and a place where an adolescent summer camper would feel quite at home. We also passed by what appeared to be the old Officers' Club, now designated as a "banquet hall" and advertised as being open for wedding parties. It seemed like a bad joke. Good cuisine just did not seem to fit this place. The truck and the ride seemed the perfect metaphor for Camp Wolters: rustic, with nothing resembling comfort.

The most striking thing about Camp Wolters during World War II was the complete absence of color or variety: the hundreds of wooden buildings were painted all white; the tens of thousands of soldiers wore either drab olive green or khaki; every car and truck was green; the terrain was all brown, and the food all grey. Essentially, Camp Wolters was a vast human assembly line, with the input raw material 18 - and 19-year-old males, many of them malnourished, and the output a monochromatic set of soldiers expected to act like robots in circumstances and places they found difficult to imagine. Now my father was one of them: a United States Army infantryman.

Writing about this time, the war correspondent Ernie Pyle described his affinity for this group of soldiers: "I love infantry because they are the underdogs. They are the mud-rain-frost-wind-boys. They have no comforts, and they even learn to live without the necessities and they in the end are the guys who wars cannot be won without."[42]

# 3
# THE 99TH

IN JANUARY 1944, AFTER COMPLETING basic training, my father was posted to Camp Maxey in Paris, Texas, northeast of Dallas. There he joined the 99th Infantry Division. The 99th "Checkerboards" earned its name from its distinctive three-rowed checkered shoulder patch with blue and white squares centered on a black shield.

The division had been at Camp Maxey for several months, undergoing advanced training prior to being sent overseas to the European theater of the war. Formed in 1942 at Camp Van Dorn, Mississippi, the 99th drew its core personnel from the Pennsylvania National Guard. After its arrival at Camp Maxey, the 99th was subsequently fleshed out with approximately 3,000 former ASTPers like my father.[43] The hard-bitten Pennsylvania toughs who formed the core of the 99th referred to the newly arrived ASTPers as "College Fucks"—a term they still jokingly used decades later at a division reunion.

Some of the ASTPers were already attending college at campuses such as Baylor University, Texas A&M, the University of North Carolina, and Georgia Tech when the Army terminated the program and shipped them off to units such as the 99th and Camp Maxey, where such combat units were forming up.

The Army's calculus at this point was simple: soldiers were needed less for their brains than for their ability to pull a trigger. The comfort of the college environment and free-spirited academic thought was traded in for the hot and sticky environment of east Texas and the immediacy of combat and killing.

Camp Maxey was situated in a part of Texas with gently rolling hills covered in scrub pine. Like many wartime camps, the installation consisted of temporary wooden barracks that were, in this instance, arrayed in a semi-circle around a lake. Also, like Camp Wolters, Camp Maxey was a colorless world of 90 degree-angle buildings devoid of anything that stood out. Its rows of box-like, two-story barracks communicated to my father and the tens of thousands of other soldiers who arrived at its gates: *don't screw up, don't stand out, and forget about being an individualist. Hunker down. Just blend in.*

Dad was assigned to "F" Company of the 394th Infantry Regiment, one of three infantry units that, along with other supporting elements, rounded out the approximately 15,000 soldiers in the division.[44] The other soldiers came from the variety of backgrounds and hometowns typical of the conscripted wartime army.

Training at Camp Maxey was intended to develop the 99th Infantry Division into a cohesive fighting force ready for its deployment overseas. The days were filled with marching and training exercises, including attacking a mock village with mock defenders. The soldiers otherwise pummeled the woods around the camp with rifle and machine gun fire, grenades, mortars, and flamethrowers. The flamethrower was a particularly creative device that spewed flaming liquid into hard-to-reach places where the enemy might be hiding. It also meant that the unfortunate soldier carrying it had to maneuver in combat with a relatively exposed gasoline tank on his back.

Dad's platoon, which comprised about 40 soldiers, was fortunate to have as its platoon sergeant "Cut" Cunningham. Cut was a young man who was all of 23 years old in 1944. My father always spoke with reverence about him as someone who was a good soldier and mentor. It was easy to see why.

Cut was part of the Pennsylvania core of the 99th. These were guys who were never labeled "College Fucks." Instead they were soldiers who, before the war, worked blue-collar jobs, and for whom attending college was an unlikely proposition. Cut had worked on the railroad before becoming a part of the wartime army. Yet, aside from the jibes, guys like Cut looked out for the ASTPers. To Cut, each ASTPer was almost like the gifted little brother: the one who was going to succeed some day, if only guys like Cut protected them from whatever the enemy might throw at them.

Cut was no doubt a real tough shit. In today's Army-speak, he would be "locked on" or "high speed." Cut would see a fair amount of combat, and he was not above slapping around a German prisoner or two. Yet, Cut was the sort of person who would write a "How are you doing?" letter to my father months after he returned stateside, wounded.

When I met him at a division reunion 57 years after my father's return, Cut was acting as the designated driver for 15 other division mates. It was if he never quite stopped playing the role of guardian of his charges. From the deference still paid him by the other veterans, decades later, it was evident that Cut had been a good soldier. He had that aura of someone who saved a lot of asses, at one time or another. One of them was probably Dad's. In his later years, though still fit, Cut was soft-spoken and had a fading memory. By then, he did not remember my father. But he sighed, "There were so many."

Sergeants such as Cut Cunningham, as any military expert will tell you, are critical to the fighting abilities of an Army unit. They are the glue that holds the unit together and makes it work. Such was the case with one of my father's other sergeants, Sergeant Frank York. Like Cut, Sergeant York was an ass-kicker and the kind of soldier you wanted on your side in a fight. He later earned a battlefield commission as an officer.

Sergeant York also stood up for his soldiers. On one occasion, as my father and the other soldiers were dragging back to camp following a long day of training in the field, a superior officer drove up and told the sergeant that the men needed to march back to camp in precise parade-ground formation. Never mind that they were training for real combat, the soldiers were supposed to march back to camp like a neat row of wind-up toys—all presumably so that an officer could look good. Sergeant York's response: *his* goddamned soldiers were not marching anywhere.

In true Sergeant York style, he got in the face of the officer to make his point. That is the kind of leader he was.

Sergeant York, however, had another side: he was a heavy drinker. He even sent junior soldiers such as my father—who didn't drink—through the beer line at the Post Exchange so that he could guzzle *their* ration of beer, too. Sergeant York had others to cover for him. That others would do so was perhaps not uncommon. After all, this was about going into mortal combat, so if the guy who was going to save your butt also happened to be something of a drunk, so be it.

Unfortunately, the competence of sergeants such as Frank York and Cut Cunningham was counterbalanced by incompetence in the senior ranks of the 99th. To this day, Dad is still incredulous about his battalion commander, a lieutenant colonel, whose overriding priority was to keep the shine on the brass pipe fittings on the battalion toilets and sinks. It was as if taking on the German Army—in 1944 still one of the finest armies in history— was something of lesser importance that could wait. This same lieutenant colonel, dropped off by his spouse in full view of the battalion, would then stand at attention and render her a formal salute. This rather weird ceremony left my father, at that time a self-admitted smart-ass, along with the other 18-year-old soldiers, unimpressed—particularly because this was the man who was going to lead them into war and perhaps death.

Dad's penchant for being a smart-ass earned him the enmity of a young lieutenant who liked to carry around a swagger stick. The swagger stick resembled a riding crop that one might use on horses rather than soldiers. One day, as the lieutenant was berating a soldier who was suffering the aftereffects of a broken ankle, my father commented within earshot that, for the lieutenant, serving in the Army was "nothing more than a meal ticket." *Strike 1*. Next, during a briefing, as the lieutenant was lecturing everyone on the importance of earning the Expert Infantryman Badge, Dad stated that he was already qualified, much to the embarrassment of the lieutenant. *Strike 2*. In a scene worthy of Hollywood, the lieutenant called my father out and asked "whether he liked ships," because he personally was going to ensure that Dad was assigned as a replacement infantryman and sent overseas to the front lines as soon as possible. Fortunately, Strike 3 never happened. The lieutenant never carried out his threat. He himself became a replacement and was sent to the front lines early, only to be killed.

Incompetence in the officer ranks of the 99th was not limited to lower-and mid-level officers. The 99th Infantry Division commander, General Walter Lauer, is probably best remembered for playing the piano during the Battle of the Bulge, the last major German combat offensive of the war and one in which the 99th would play a critical role. In perhaps a foretaste of General Lauer's detachment, or less charitably, failure to "get it," Dad recalled the general giving a speech to the division before departing Camp Maxey. He insisted that the soldiers in the 99th were going to win more medals than anyone else. After a quick calculation — no doubt by many of the ASTPers — the troops figured out that more medals meant that more of them would be killed and maimed. Therefore, they promptly booed the general. His motivational "rah-rah" was not going to work with this crowd.

The mood of the soldiers in booing the general was perfectly summed up in Joseph Heller's seminal work about the war, *Catch 22*: "The enemy is anybody who's going to get you killed, no matter which side he is on."[45] In retrospect, the ineptness of General Lauer and some of the other officers my father encountered was not entirely surprising. Throughout American history, rapidly stood-up wartime armies included in their ranks leaders who, under other circumstances, never would have been promoted into leadership positions.

While at Camp Maxey, my father also underwent sniper training. This meant learning to kill with a single rifle shot at long distances. Dad grew up hunting and was a deadeye shot. Decades later, he still talked with boy-like enthusiasm about having the opportunity to shoot a 1903 Springfield bolt-action rifle equipped with a Weaver scope, and hitting targets at ranges of up to a mile. My father had the chance to show off his prowess to a visiting general by hitting a distant target during a demonstration, much to the relief of the nervous lieutenant supervising the training.

A demonstration that did not go so well was the day the division was lined up to witness an amphibious vehicle crossing a local lake. The vehicle sank during the demonstration. This did not inspire confidence among the soldiers. Luckily, the 99th never used these vehicles in combat.

---

At Camp Maxey, my father was also introduced to another aspect of Army life — anti-Semitism. Like his previous exposure to segregation at Camp Wolters, as a small town Iowan, anti-Semitism was entirely new to my father, and he was very much taken aback. In this case, some soldiers voiced their conviction that Jewish soldiers were "dogging it" — slang for not pulling their weight. The theory went, if the Jewish soldiers couldn't, or wouldn't do their part, how could they be trustworthy in combat? Some of the non-commissioned officers were complicit in fostering this attitude. The label "Jew boy" and other derogatory epitaphs seemed to be a standard part of their vocabulary.

Such attitudes were not limited to soldiers in the 99th. They pervaded the U.S. Army throughout the war — and throughout the country. How the Army could get this so spectacularly wrong is unfathomable. For all the emphasis placed on patriotism, democratic values, and unit cohesion, it seems alien that the U.S. Army could countenance the biases some soldiers brought into the service from civilian life; biases that infected the preparations for the deadly serious business of war. Ironically, it was a war fought against a foe who carried out the systematic slaughter of Jewish men, women, and children. It was a slaughter that was so depraved and on so monstrous a scale as to be incomprehensible.

Less than a year later, and after five months of combat and over 6,500 battle casualties — including over 1,100 dead — the 99th liberated the Mühldorf concentration camp complex in southern Bavaria.[46] They found almost 1,500 Jews living under barbaric conditions. The Mühldorf camp housed Hungarian Jews as well as those from Greece, France, and Italy, along with political prisoners, all of whom were forced to work in the German defense industry. Periodically, the Nazi guards carried out "selections" of workers who were too ill or unfit. These workers were deported to the Auschwitz concentration camp to be gassed. Other Jews were shot on site. Some were just allowed to die of neglect as part of a premeditated and systematic ethnic cleansing.[47]

The 99th was later recognized by the U.S. Army and the United States Holocaust Memorial Museum in Washington, D.C. as a liberating unit.[48] For those soldiers in the 99th who, less than a year before, may have harbored anti-Semitic views, the experience likely cast such prejudice in an entirely different light.

---

Today, little is left of the infrastructure of Camp Maxey except the stone pillars on either side of the main entrance. The pillars appear as silent sentries, and were likely my father's first glimpse of the place as he stepped off the train from the adjacent railroad track. The site reveals little of its past. The barracks are long gone, although part of the old reservation is still used by the Texas National Guard for training.

While visiting, I encountered one of the two-soldier caretaker garrison jogging down the road. She graciously showed me the small but well-kept and informative camp museum, depicting the base's history as a training site for the 99th and 102nd Infantry Divisions. The last entry in the dusty museum guestbook was from 1955. Stepping outside and surveying the ground, I experienced a feeling I often had in visiting the places my father had been—that it was hard to imagine that a small slice of his history was here. Perhaps this was because what was left of Camp Maxey was barren, peaceful, and far away from anything. It seemed hard to envisage it as a staging ground for the defining event of the 20th century that was World War II.

Camp Maxey, like Camp Wolters, was a tough environment that was not for the faint-hearted. But it was ideal for someone like my father in 1944—young, confident and, perhaps, fearless. The fact that my father recalled comical incidents at Camp Maxey reminded me that he was remembering events as an 18-year-old less than a year out of high school. During this period, though, he learned perhaps one of the most primitive and ghastly human skills—the ability to unflinchingly kill other humans. Once switched on, such skills and the associated memories could never entirely be switched off.

---

During my father's training at Camp Maxey, his father, Ben Wedewer, was killed in an instance of being in the wrong place at the wrong time. While pulled over on the side of Highway 20, about 10 miles west of Dubuque, Iowa, he was run over by bootleggers running cheap liquor into Iowa. Apparently, they mistook him for the local sheriff. Although Ben Wedewer was not a particularly high-profile citizen of the community, his death nonetheless made the front page of the April 12, 1944, edition of the Waterloo, Iowa, *Daily Courier*.[49] My father was allowed a week's leave to attend the funeral.

I have a photo in my office of my father at age 18, dressed in the uniform of a U.S. Army Private, holding the hand of his niece. It was taken around the time he buried his father. He is tall, slender, and doesn't look particularly like a fearsome warrior ready for the horrors of war. No matter. Ready or not, my father was headed to a rendezvous with his destiny—and, like his father, of being in the wrong place at the wrong time.

# 4

# ACROSS THE ATLANTIC

AFTER CAMP MAXEY, THE NEXT stop for my father was Camp Myles Standish near Taunton, Massachusetts. The camp essentially served as a staging area for troops prior to shipping out overseas. From there, the 99th Division was sent by truck and train to Boston, arriving at the South Street Station on September 28 and 29, 1944, for embarkation in the ships that would take them across the Atlantic to England. For Dad, it was the USAT (United States Army Transport) *Exchequer*, a converted cargo ship now serving as a troopship. He and several hundred other soldiers were packed into a vessel approximately 490 feet long by 69 feet wide[50] — a size that would be dwarfed by a modern cruise liner. The ship itself had high, vaulted sides and a superstructure and smokestack in the middle. In appearance, the *Exchequer* was essentially a floating warehouse with a bow and a stern. But now, instead of carrying bulk cargoes such as wheat or soybeans, it was crammed with soldiers in canvas bunks tied between poles and stacked four high.

Soon after boarding the *Exchequer*, Dad had his first encounter with the face of war — literally. Some of the ship's crew were survivors of vessels sunk by German submarines. Their faces had been so badly burned by the flaming oil through which they swam to survive, my father couldn't bear to look at them. This was the first real image of war he saw, and it was not the sanitized version in the propagandistic training films. Instead, this was the sort of haunting image that, once downloaded into the recipient's brain, could never be erased, no matter how hard he or she tried. After seeing this real, disturbing face of war, my father wondered how, with such seemingly debilitating injuries, these people could keep going.

———⋙○⋘———

The 99th sailed from Boston on the evening of September 29, 1944, on board five ships. They were part of a small convoy that included escort ships intended to defend them against German submarines, or so-called U-boats. The term U-boat was English slang for the German designation "Unterseeboot" (undersea boat). Such vessels were known to prowl off the U.S. coast, at times within sight of shore, and were bent on destroying cargo ships and troopships before they were able to reach the war in Europe. During World War II, as soon as a ship departed an East Coast port, it was a potential target for the feared U-boats, which would strike without warning. In the disfigured faces of *Exchequer* crewmembers, Dad had seen the U-boat's ability to kill and injure.

Soon after leaving Boston, the *Exchequer* joined a larger convoy, designated CU-41, which sailed from New York around the same time. The "CU" prefix indicated that the convoy carried fuel supplies in oil tankers that originally sailed from Curacao in the Dutch West Indies. The good news for the troops was that CU-41 was a faster-moving convoy, at 13 to 14 knots.[51] This meant it had a better chance of evading the U-boats. Thirteen to 14 knots—or about 17 to 18 miles per hour—was not particularly fast, but it was better than the nine miles per hour of the slower-moving convoys. The threat from U-boats, even relatively late in the war, was something everyone took seriously. Approximately three months later, for example, a Boston convoy was ambushed as it was about to enter the Canadian port of Halifax.[52] In less than half an hour, three of the convoy's ships were torpedoed and subsequently sunk or beached. It was the sea-going equivalent of a killing spree—a spree that only ended when one of the frantic escort vessels smashed into the marauding U-boat.[53] The U-boat escaped, nonetheless.[54]

As Dad stood on deck, he counted more than 50 U.S. and Allied ships in CU-41. They included tankers, troopships, cargo ships,

# THE BRAVEST GUY

and a small British aircraft carrier, HMS *Patroller*, its deck stacked with aircraft being ferried overseas.[55] The convoy was escorted by nine destroyer escorts and a lead destroyer, the USS *Winslow*. These were much smaller ships, armed with deck guns and other weapons that could defend against the prowling U-boats.[56]

As was characteristic of World War II, and perhaps recent wars, many of these escorting ships from the U.S. Navy and Coast Guard were named after young people killed in the war—young people who had no inkling that someday a ship would be named after them. There was the USS *Finch*, named after Lieutenant Joseph Warren Finch, Jr., killed in the Pacific war at age 22; the USS *Ramsden*, named after 23-year-old Marvin Lee Ramsden of Pleasant Lake, North Dakota, a Navy sailor killed at 23 in the Pacific war; the USS *Rhodes*, named after Navy Ensign Allison Phidel Rhodes, born in Walhalla, South Carolina, and killed at 23 in the Pacific war; the USS *Richey*, named after 21-year-old Navy Ensign Joseph Lee Richey, a naval aviator from Barnard, Missouri, killed during the Japanese attack on Pearl Harbor. And there was the USS *Sellstrom*, named after Navy Ensign Edward Robert Sellstrom, from Gowrie, Iowa—a naval aviator and winner of the Navy Cross for bravery, killed at 25.[57] Even in the North Atlantic, where grey sea blended with grey sky, and upon which the grey ships of convoy CU-41 bobbed in an inexorable, plodding journey east, the war, in a way, brought two Iowans together: Navy hero Robert Sellstrom, in the form of a ship named after him, and Don Wedewer, a 19-year-old infantryman seeing war for the first time. Neither ever expected to be there.

Overall, Convoy CU-41 was a cross between a covered wagon train of frontier days, accompanied by cavalry troops, and a battering ram meant to push through whatever hazards the Germans or nature may have placed in its path. The convoy occupied several square miles of ocean, and the ships were positioned in parallel columns that zigged and zagged back and forth. The idea was to spoil a submarine's aim by steering an uneven course resembling that of a student driver behind the wheel for the first time. Years later, when in my own career I was impressed by the sight of 20 naval ships together, I could only imagine the awe that would have been felt by a teenager from eastern Iowa in seeing more than twice that number. Such moments would no doubt have made my father realize he was a part of something much larger. It was also a far cry from the dusty fields of Texas, fighting against a make-believe enemy.

Now the war became real. In embarking across the North Atlantic, the soldiers of the 99th entered a war zone where submarine-launched torpedoes or mines could break a ship in half and send it to the bottom in minutes. Sixteen months earlier, the USAT *Dorchester*, had been torpedoed by a U-boat off Greenland. More than 650 had died, including many soldiers who froze to death in the icy waters.[58] Even if you survived a torpedo blast in the North Atlantic, you were likely to die from hypothermia—a death prefaced by uncontrollable shaking and gradual numbness.

The hazards faced by CU-41, though, were not all human-made. The seas during the 99th's early October 1944 crossing were unceasingly rough. As a result, nearly everyone was seasick and eager to get some fresh air on deck. The men occasionally vomited into woolen winter caps, which were tossed over the side, or into their trusty, reusable helmets, thus leaving a trail of vomit in the *Exchequer*'s wake. After seeing a fellow soldier throw up, another chided, "I thought you had a strong stomach."

The curt response: "I do. See, I threw it a long way."

When not recovering in the fresh air, soldiers marked time in the stale, fetid air below decks. It's a unique smell, produced by a combination of body odor, military equipment, too much paint, and a lack of ventilation. During the almost two-week-long voyage in the cramped quarters of the *Exchequer*, there was little to do other than write letters, read, play cards, and eat—while standing—one of the two daily meals. One soldier from the 99th later recalled that he and some of the other soldiers were so hungry after the meager meals that they begged a cook for a little bit of something else—anything. The cook's response: "Here, have an onion sandwich."[59] As a break from the monotony of the voyage, the soldiers were also able to listen to part of the baseball World Series over loudspeakers.

On the eighth day out, explosions sounded in the distance as the escorting ships dropped depth charges into the ocean around the convoy. The depth charge was essentially a garbage can packed with explosives, which the escort ships lobbed into the ocean in an attempt to destroy or deter lurking U-boats, which may or may not have been there. As they exploded, the depth charges created arching plumes of water.

In one sense, whether the enemy was real or imagined didn't matter, because with the U-boats you never could be sure.

As a result of the rough seas, even those sailors responsible for the ship's defense became seasick, and as a result some of the 99th's soldiers took over manning the deck guns. Because the *Exchequer* was armed with larger deck guns and thus considered more capable of defending itself, it was, at one point, placed in the outer, most exposed column of ships. Here the *Exchequer* was exceedingly vulnerable. With a single torpedo a U-boat could have sent the ship and hundreds of soldiers to their deaths in minutes. Whether it was due to the *Exchequer's* exposed position or the thought of combat in Europe that awaited them, my father noticed that nearly everyone attended church services.

Decades later, a 99th veteran recalled that the ship in which he crossed the Atlantic began with an "E." By perhaps odd coincidence, most of the ships carrying the 99th had names that began with an E. In any case, he did not care to remember the name of the ship or the miserable voyage.[60]

# 5

# ENGLAND

Although the North Atlantic crossing was uncomfortable, Convoy CU-41 came through unscathed. After landing in Gourock, Scotland, on October 11, 1944, the soldiers of the 99th were dispersed to staging areas around the south of England in preparation for movement to the European continent. For the 394th Infantry Regiment and my father, this meant temporary billets in small hotels in Lyme Regis, a coastal town in the southwestern county of Dorset. With its quaint streets, Lyme Regis resembled a small village rather than a military installation.

Even in this relatively idyllic setting, my father saw more disturbing images of war. This time it was the forlorn faces of kids who had been removed from their homes and parents in London to escape the incessant bombing. In those kids' faces my father saw the sadness, loneliness, and uncertainty of a world gone crazy; a world bereft of any real normalcy. Perhaps in typical American fashion, the soldiers gave the kids candy and other trinkets. It was a small act of humanity in a world where there seemed so little of it — a world in which the terror bombing of cities had, by 1944, taken on an even more horrific form.

Dad's brief stay in Lyme Regis also introduced him, albeit indirectly, to another aspect of wartime life — widespread prostitution. He was assigned to guard the local "house," which was above a drug store. The "businesswomen" who taunted my father and the other guards were off-limits to the American soldiers, because the women were not certified by the government as being "safe" from sexually transmitted diseases. To prevent sex-starved soldiers from nonetheless doing business there, someone in authority felt the need to guard the place. So one of the first assignments my father—the innocent Catholic teenager from Iowa—undertook, was guard duty at the local house of ill repute.

---

During this time, Dad was granted a three-day recreational leave. Along with two other soldiers from his rifle squad, Ed Walz and Bill Tipton, he used it to take the train to London. In my father's words, they had a "swell time." Like Dad, Walz and Tipton had been in the Army ASTP. They were headed for college—or were already there—until the need for front-line soldiers changed their plans. All were young, straight-arrow guys brought together by shared experience and unspoken anxiety about their futures.

In London, they stayed at the "George Washington Hotel." This wasn't its real name—it was one of a number of British hotels that were taken over to accommodate visiting American troops, and given Americanized names. Accommodations for my father and his companions consisted of bunk beds in a single room. It was not luxurious, but it was better than what they were accustomed to in Army life.

As welcome as the break was, Dad saw more of the reality of the war when he, Walz, and Tipton toured the city. Bomb craters and rubble were everywhere, the result of more than four years of German aerial bombardment. And in 1944, the bombardment had taken on a new, perhaps even more terrifying form through long-range rocket attacks.

During the bombings (known as the "Blitz"), many Londoners slept in underground train stations. Nothing was spared from the aerial attacks. Even London's many historic buildings were targets—structures such as the historic, domed St. Paul's Cathedral, which, as my father saw, had holes blasted in its roof.

Dad and the others also spent time at Rainbow Corner, a cavernous serviceman's club in the heart of London run 24 hours a day by the Red Cross. There, service members could eat, dance, and hang out while playing games, including one where you took target practice shooting Hitler in the mouth.

## The Bravest Guy

One of the highlights of my father's trip to London was dinner at an upscale restaurant complete with well-groomed waiters in dinner jackets. The meal itself, however, was less impressive, consisting of a piece of tough, wartime-rationed beef with the consistency of shoe leather. While there, Dad saw the famous actor Jimmy Stewart in the bar. An A-list Hollywood actor before the war, Stewart was now serving as a bomber pilot with the U.S. Army Air Force in England, from where he flew combat missions over Europe. The fact that Jimmy Stewart, a successful movie actor before and after the war, served in combat was something that perhaps made World War II different. It was total war. A war where it seemed as if everyone found a way to serve, no matter what his or her station in life—A-list actor or not.

Aside from the leather-like beef, the war also intruded on dinner in the form of distant, muffled explosions from German V-2 rockets smashing into London. The V-2 rocket was a more advanced cousin of the smaller, cruder V-1 weapon. At this point in the war, London and its surroundings were terrorized by these telephone-pole sized weapons as the Germans hurled them indiscriminately at England. It was a desperate attempt by the Germans to reverse the course of the war—a war that Germany increasingly was losing—by instilling terror.

By now, London and other British cities were accustomed to aerial bombardment by manned bomber aircraft. What made the V-1 and the V-2 different—and more terrifying—was that they flew faster and, in the case of the V-2, much higher than the bombers. With little or no warning, an entire city block could be shredded by these weapons. The V-1 could only be stopped through heavily concentrated defenses—and even then some still came through. One measure used by the Allies was to employ fighter aircraft such as the famed British Spitfire to chase down the V-1, and using the fighter aircraft's wing, flip the stubby V-1's wing over, sending the latter spiraling downward. Similarly, Allied ground forces overran German launch sites in Holland following the invasion of the continent in June 1944. In response, specially equipped German Heinkel 111 bombers launched V-1s at England while trying to evade Allied fighter aircraft. To this deadly cycle of measures and counter-measures—all too familiar in recent wars—the Germans added the V-2, which, with its superior speed, trajectory and height, was unstoppable.

The waiter at my father's table tried to explain away the distant explosions as construction-related "blasting." Dad and his companions knew better. Nevertheless, the dinner of almost inedible beef proceeded, with the muffled explosions adding to the atmosphere. At least the restaurant was ornate. And, other than retreating underground, there was nothing you could do to protect yourself from the rockets anyway. Indeed, that was the London that Wedewer, Tipton and Walz experienced. It was in one sense an almost surreal place, full of contradictions; a place where you could take taxis and buses everywhere, hang out at a club, eat a meal, see the famous sights, and, if you were so disposed, find sex. Yet, London was also a place where no one was safe from the terror, where death and destruction were everywhere, and where people were sleeping in the subway tunnels to escape the bombing. London was desperately trying to hold on to some shred of normalcy, in spite of the ever more horrific V-1 and V-2 attacks—as if more horror were possible in the fifth year of a World War.

It was. A month later, one of the flying bombs came crashing down in the London suburb of Deptford, destroying a Woolworth's department store and a co-op next door. The buildings were filled with shoppers, mostly women and small children, who were there to buy aluminum saucepans—a rarity due to the rationing of metals during the war. When the rocket hit with a tremendous roar, "the walls of the Woolworth store bulged outward, then the building collapsed" while next door, the co-op "disintegrated."[61] The simple act of shopping for something as innocuous as a saucepan turned into slaughter. The official toll was 160 killed, 77 seriously injured, 122 slightly wounded, and 11 missing.[62] The actual toll, though, was likely much higher, as the injured were rushed to hospitals before an accurate count could be made.[63] The terror attack on Deptford was another example of the slaughter of innocents by the flying bombs. More such slaughter was yet to come.

## 6

# TO THE FRONT LINES

AFTER A BRIEF RESPITE IN England, where the 99th Infantry Division reconstituted and reformed, my father took another, briefer voyage across rough waters—this time across the turbulent English Channel in a U.S. Coast Guard Landing Ship Tank, or LST. Approximately 328-feet long, the LST was not known for its creature comforts. Shaped like a shoebox, it disgorged its cargo through massive doors on its bow.[64] As on the earlier Atlantic crossing, the wind and rain on November 6 and 7, 1944, made nearly everyone on the Channel crossing seasick, including the LST's Coast Guard crew. A plodding craft in the first place, the LST's progress was further slowed by the need to avoid sea mines, as unremitting a concern as the U-boats. The approximately 100-mile transit across the English Channel was unmercifully protracted, lasting about a day.

When the ship eventually landed in Le Havre, the troops found recent fighting had left the port a shambles. Bulldozers cleared the rubble and possibly human remains so that the 99th could debark and move by truck through northern France. The rain continued as they approached the front lines on the Belgian-German border, where it turned to snow.

Belgium, in a sense, is like three countries. The western part is French-speaking, the central part Flemish, and a small slice of the eastern tip is more like Germany and is dotted with towns and villages, some with German-sounding names. My father's unit arrived in this eastern part, near the village of Wirtzfeld, on November 11. I visited Wirtzfeld some 57 years later and found it like many villages in this part of Belgium—little more than a quaint crossroads situated between a few well-kept homes with large, overhanging trees. There was an old stone Catholic church that was likely there in 1944, though a more modern inn for tourists traveling through on sightseeing buses has been added since then. The village lies in a bucolic, postcard-like setting surrounded by rolling hayfields interspersed with forest.

Wirtzfeld was close enough to the front lines to require patrolling, in case the Germans attempted to infiltrate the area from their positions further east. My father and his patrol mate, Chuck Runland of Seattle, were assigned to scout the edge of the woods near Wirtzfeld. At six feet, six inches, Runland cut an imposing figure. He was about four inches taller than my father, although Dad insisted this didn't make Runland any better on the basketball court. At basketball, my father recalled, "Runland was lousy."

Basketball talent didn't much matter now, though. As the pair set out on one of their first combat assignments, they likely avoided thinking how slim their chances were of emerging from combat unscathed. Before the Normandy invasion, planners estimated that infantrymen would comprise 70 percent of the killed, wounded, or missing. By August 1944, they'd raised that estimate to 83 percent.[65] In the end, because three of every four casualties occurred in rifle platoons, those units sustained 90 percent of the Army's losses in Europe during the war.[66]

Unaware of these stark statistics, my father and Runland set out. Dad carried an M-1 rifle, his favored weapon because it was semi-automatic, reliable, relatively accurate, and simple. "I could take it apart and reassemble it with my eyes closed," he later claimed. Perhaps, like all infantryman before and since, he formed a bond with his trusty M-1. Much like the relationship between a pilot and plane, or a sailor and ship, the infantryman respected his rifle because he needed it to bring him home. Runland carried a Browning Automatic Rifle, or BAR, a big hulking fully automatic weapon with a bipod on the front. Like the later M-60 machine gun, the BAR could do some real damage, or at least scare the enemy. Its slow, staccato, boom-boom-boom could also alert your buddies that you were in trouble.

At dusk on November 11, the snow was falling fast and piling up, creating a Christmas card-like scene around Wirtzfeld: rolling hills blanketed by snow, tall pine trees with frosted limbs in the distance, an occasional tidy barn or house with white-capped, sloping roofs dotting the landscape. Runland and my father, however, gave little thought to the scenery—there was a war on.

Even with vast armies and fortifications arrayed against each other in this sector, the war came down to this—a two-man patrol of inexperienced 19-year-olds patrolling an area of about a square mile. It was probably a far larger area than they could watch over. Their sleeping quarters that night were haystacks. When they awoke in the morning, they and their equipment were covered in snow, and Dad lost a hand grenade. At that point, Runland saw soldiers in the distance and prepared to fire his BAR, until discovering they were from their own G Company. My father and Runland also discovered something else: footprints in the snow not far from where they'd slept, indicating the possible presence of German patrols that likely would have overwhelmed them had they been spotted.

After those near misses, three days later, on November 14, 1944, my father and F Company moved east to just inside Germany as part of a general movement of the 394th Infantry Regiment. The 394th was positioned along a four-mile line east of Honsfeld, Belgium, across the German border. Here, F Company occupied about a 1,200-yard segment of the northern portion of the 394th's lines.[67,68]

It was an ironic twist. More than 70 years after Dad's grandfather, "Barney" Wedewer, left Germany because he was sick of war—sick of the killing, sick of the maiming, and sick of the destruction—his grandson was back in Germany engaged in the same deadly business. My father grew up with things German—the German language, German culture, German food, and a German name. Yet, in the deadly business of war, he had absolutely no hesitation in killing Germans.

The forest in this part of Belgium is called the Ardennes, also known as the Hürtgen forest on the German side of the border. During my visit there decades later, it seemed a forest like no other. Even on a cloudless, bright summer afternoon, the tree cover is so thick it's like entering a dark room. There is little undergrowth, just densely packed, tall pine trees that blot out the sun. The forest is bisected by a number of logging roads and fire breaks, which attest to its still productive use. The other memorable feature of the forest is its silence. It is almost impenetrable by sound; even the rumbling of logging trucks close by can barely be heard.

The Ardennes under several feet of snow in 1944 was an eerie, almost surreal place to wage war. The sky was always grey, the scenery a wintry panorama of black and white. It snowed and rained constantly in what turned out to be a very wet winter. The Ardennes seemed unsuitable for the movement of large masses of soldiers and material. Instead, this environment seemed better suited to small-unit actions, or probing enemy defensive positions along the Siegfried Line.

The Siegfried Line was constructed by the Germans to stop a further Allied advance eastward. It consisted of a series of fearsome, low-lying fortifications just inside the German border, no more than a thousand yards from the American positions. In aggregate, this was claustrophobic combat.

This was my father's reality as a 19-year-old foot soldier, an Army Private First Class paid $59 a month. In terms of grand movements or offensives, the front was relatively stagnant in the Ardennes at this point in the war, with the major advances being made in other sectors. According to intelligence reports, the German troops faced by the 99th on its arrival were a motley collection of old men, young boys, and naval troops conscripted from a German Navy that had largely ceased to exist.

If the German personnel initially facing the 99th were decidedly rag-tag, their weaponry was not. In the Ardennes, the Germans had deployed a formidable array of weapons which, combined with the environment, threatened the soldiers of the 99th with a peculiar set of horrors. There were the fearsome "Nebelwerfer" rockets, shot in bunches into the treetops above the Americans, that flew with a cascading, ear-splitting roar that earned them the nickname "Screaming Mimis." On impacting the treetops, the Screaming Mimis sprayed shrapnel (metal fragments) in a canopy-like pattern that shredded unarmored, exposed American soldiers.

There were barely visible "pillboxes" — concrete machine gun nests burrowed into the ground by the Germans, from which unsuspecting American patrols would be annihilated. There were the German "burp guns" — small, lethal submachine guns that compensated for whatever combat prowess the Germans' second – and third-tier soldiers may have lacked. There were the equally deadly German 88-millimeter cannons, which were perfect for blasting the tops off trees, and combined with the Screaming Mimis to shower the vulnerable Americans with a hailstorm of scissor-like steel shards.

And then there were the mines and booby traps. Taking advantage of the densely packed trees, the Germans infested the Ardennes with these devices — the goddamned things were everywhere. The Germans already had a reputation as world leaders in innovative weapon design, and lived up to this standard when it came to devising booby traps and mines. They would often string piano wire with dynamite on either end between trees, hoping to ensnare an unsuspecting infantryman. The blast from this device was intended to tear an unarmored body in half. Equally horrific were the "Bouncing Betties" that carpeted the forest floor. When stepped on, these mines would click and then pop into the air before exploding at groin height. To this toxic mix, the Germans added pressure contact mines made of wood or plastic that evaded detection by minesweeping equipment.

Little in my father's and his fellow soldiers' training or equipment prepared them for how to deal with these horrors. The only training they received was in how to stick their knives under a mine in the hope of exposing it. Plainly this method was unsuited for the snow-covered, frozen ground of the Ardennes.

Of all the horrors they faced at this point, the mines and booby traps were the deadliest. The Germans effectively transformed this formerly idyllic forest filled with majestic trees, into a frightening labyrinth of maiming and death.

As well as dealing with the Germans' attempts to kill them, the Americans also had to contend with nature: temperatures in the 20s, intermittent snow, and considerable rain. These elements combined to produce a damp chilliness that was magnified by the soldiers' lack of proper footwear. This in turn led to the aptly named trench foot, a condition resulting from prolonged exposure of the feet to moisture, which soaked through boots that were without overshoes and unsuited to the winter environment in the Ardennes. In its advanced stages, trench foot turned a soldier's feet into a gelatinous mess of open sores and pus that could lead to amputation and permanent disability.

After almost three years of war — not to mention the lessons of World War I — it seemed obvious that the Army chain of command should have recognized trench foot as a problem, and that they would have supplied soldiers with proper footwear. They didn't. As a result, the soldiers were woefully underequipped, and the impacts on some units were devastating. In November 1944, one infantry regiment engaged near the 99th evacuated more than 500 soldiers as casualties from trench foot and exposure during the first four days of one engagement.[69] This exceeded the number of actual battle casualties. In another infantry regiment, one company of more than 100 soldiers had only 14 soldiers available for duty, chiefly because of casualties from trench foot.[70] The situation was so desperate in one Army unit that men whose feet were too swollen from trench foot to permit them to walk were carried by their comrades to forward foxholes.[71] As one Army medical history observed, trench foot became a plague caused in large part by bad decision making in the Quartermaster Corps that, however unwittingly, aided and abetted the enemy in literally taking the feet out from under the U.S. Army in Europe.[72]

This occurrence was eerily similar to the recent failure in Iraq to supply soldiers with proper body armor and armored vehicles, and was caused in part by the same thinking: the war would be over soon, and such provisions or planning were unnecessary. Like the failures in Iraq, the failure to provide soldiers in the European theater with proper footwear was scandalous, and an Army medical report later lamented, "There is no real excuse."[73]

---

Life on the front lines was mostly lived in foxholes—two-man dugouts, about four to five feet deep and rimmed with logs and dirt. From their foxholes, my father and the other soldiers occasionally glimpsed the random German several hundred yards away. Sometimes they took a shot, hoping to kill one. As is meticulously detailed in the 394th Infantry Regiment's after-action reports, this seemed like a war of shadows, with soldiers on each side catching fleeting glimpses of the enemy in the wintry gloom framed by the dense, snow-caked forest. Movement consisted of small, probing patrols intended to get a better idea of where the enemy was, and, if possible, kill or capture a German.

It didn't take long. On November 14, 1944, one of my father's F Company mates, Private First Class Edwin Snyder, claimed the regiment's first kill. While admiring a buddy's sniper rifle, he spotted a German about a thousand yards away and promptly shot him through the throat.[74] The unlucky German had stepped out of his pillbox to smoke his pipe. The picture of his frozen corpse, still clutching his throat, with his pipe and tobacco pouch at his side, is prominently displayed in the regimental after-action report.[75] Later on, the first German soldier captured by the regiment was caught walking down a road toward a village on the other side of the American lines. Apparently, the German was on furlough and did not realize that his destination was already in the hands of the Americans.[76]

---

Other than the snow and cold, one constant that my father recalled on the front lines was the shelling from the Screaming

Mimis and 88s. It was incessant, day and night. The night shelling was the worst. In the evening, the shells came with increasing frequency, perhaps as an attempt by the Germans to demoralize the Americans by depriving them of sleep. For Private Wedewer and others, being shelled at night was like being in a blacked-out room buffeted by a ferocious storm. As the shells exploded in the treetops, fragments sprayed everywhere. The shells' impact also set off a further cacophony of crashes and blasts, as snow-laden branches fell to earth and in turn detonated booby traps and mines. This produced an odd rhythm of sorts — boom, crash, crash, crash, boom crash, crash, crash, boom, crash, crash, crash. Added to this racket was the occasional roar of German V-1 robot bombs zooming overhead to slaughter unsuspecting soldiers or families behind the front lines.

Throughout all the shelling and noise, the foxhole was my father's refuge. There were two soldiers to a foxhole. My father's foxhole buddy was a guy named Hahn, from Nebraska. Dad considered it fortuitous that he had not drawn as his buddy his former patrol mate Runland — he was concerned that Runland's six foot, six inch frame presented too inviting a target that would get them both killed. At night, my father and Hahn rotated two hours on duty and two hours off, to grab some sleep. Some 68 years later, Dad was still a little incredulous, insisting that Hahn had cheated him in slicing some time off *his* two hours.

The foxhole was also where my father ate D-bars. The D-bar was a horrible chocolate concoction purposely formulated to taste like a boiled potato. Some called it "Hitler's secret weapon."[77] There were also K-rations, which were beans heated by Sterno cans. If you wanted a more elaborate meal, i.e. some gruel heated up in a mess pot about 100 yards behind the front lines, you could run for it and hope you weren't shot by a German sniper. In some ways, life in the Ardennes was not unlike life in recent wars, at some outpost in Iraq or Afghanistan, where you could easily be killed doing the ordinary things in life, like grabbing a meal, writing a letter, taking a smoke break, or taking a shit.

This existence led soldiers to improvise. For example, the

Sterno cans used to heat beans were great for drying out socks. This was crucial to prevent trench foot. Similarly, the soldiers' steel helmets doubled as great portable toilets.

My father's experience in the foxhole was punctuated by the occasional forward patrol to scout enemy positions, in what was termed an "active defense of assigned zone."[78] During these patrols, he sometimes served as "Scout 1" or "Scout 2." This meant my father was the lead soldier, whose role was euphemistically described as "to seek to force enemy riflemen and machine guns to disclose their position."[79] In effect, Dad was cannon fodder — the soldier who would get shot or blown up first, should the patrol encounter concealed German positions or the ubiquitous mines and booby traps. On one of these patrols, thinking that the faster he ran the less likely he was to be shot, and likely fueled by adrenaline and fear, Dad scouted too far ahead of the patrol, earning a rebuke from his squad leader. By my father's calculation, getting so far ahead of the other soldiers put him, at least briefly, at the spear point of the Allied advance into Germany.

While he shot at the Germans a few times, Dad did not recall killing any of them. When asked about how the other soldiers handled this kind of war, his response was that some did and some did not. Some soldiers asked for a Section 8, which was a plea to return to the rear area for psychological reasons. Others resorted to self-inflicted wounds, for example, one guy told Dad, "I want to get trench foot." Risking amputation — anything to escape his debilitating fear — this soldier was successful in turning his feet into jelly-like, oozing mounds of flesh. He was soon gone. And my father would encounter at least one other soldier seeking to avoid combat. This gnawing fear and willingness to do anything to escape it was contrary to the popularized image of World War II as a grand endeavor in which this sort of thing didn't happen. It did.

Overall, Dad's and the other soldiers' existence on the front lines was a mixture of a battle against the elements — the constant cold, wet, slush and discomfort — and the equally debilitating, psychological toll of constantly being on edge, caused by the knowledge that you could be killed or maimed at any time by an array of unseen, horrific weapons employed by a faceless, hated enemy. The Army's campaign in Europe during World War II was later likened to a "Crusade in Europe" on a grand scale.[80] However, to the teenagers on the front lines, like my father, it probably did not feel much like a grand anything.

---

Even with the horrors he faced, Dad maintained his characteristic unflappability. Writing home on November 17, 1944, "in my foxhole somewhere on the front in Germany," he observed, "It is pretty cold here already and we have plenty of snow. However as long as I keep my feet dry and have enough to eat, I think I can stand the weather and the Jerrys."[81] Dad's advice to his brother Eddy, who had also been drafted into the Army, was to "take advantage of all of those civilian luxuries such as big meals." He closed with the plea, "Please pray… Love Don."[82]

# 7

# WOUNDED

On November 20, 1944, my father's infantry company was tasked with a combat patrol ahead of their positions and in the vicinity of three German pillboxes. The pillboxes formed a salient in the American lines. Dad was dressed in olive-colored drab, heavy wool fatigues, a field jacket, leggings (an anachronistic decorative boot covering left over from an earlier era), and a steel helmet. He was carrying his standard M-1 rifle and grenades. Dad had no body armor. For the average World War II soldier, there wasn't any. He looked as young as his 19 years, stood about six feet one-and-a-half inches, and weighed about 155 pounds. The weather was typically cold and overcast, with around two feet of snow on the ground.

As the members of my father's patrol prepared to set out, one of the soldiers said he didn't want to go. Perhaps it was the constant shelling. Perhaps it was the booby traps. Perhaps it was the mines, or the pillboxes, or the V-1s roaring overhead, or the enemy snipers, all of which were made worse by the numbing cold; wet, crappy food, and sleeplessness. Maybe this toxic, grinding combination of constant fatigue and fear unnerved him. In any case, this soldier did not want to go. And he didn't, while my father and the rest of the soldiers set out into the gloom.

Soon after setting out, things went horribly wrong. A soldier up ahead, Private Mazellen, triggered a booby trap that blew parts of his chest through his back. Then, a sergeant named DiSanto was cut down when another booby trap exploded. The medic (medical orderly), Technician Fifth Grade Harold Viet, went ahead to treat him and soon called for help.[83] Dad volunteered to go. As the unit was to learn, this was the wrong way to proceed, because where there was one booby trap or mine, there were others.[84] It would have been better for the rescuing soldiers to first establish a path to the injured soldier clear of booby traps, to avoid further injury in the rescue effort.[85] But everyone was new, and one of their own was badly injured and needed help—now. It was not a moment of cool, deliberate, analytical thought.

What happened next is unclear. Approaching the medic, my father saw that Sergeant DiSanto had a leg wound. As he looked around for a tree branch to use as a splint, he likely walked around the roots at the base of a tree or the edge of a path. Both were prime areas where the Germans planted mines and booby traps.

There was an explosion. Whether Dad's or Viet's movements triggered the explosion is uncertain. It was probably my father. Most likely, he stepped on a contact mine, the blast from which did its horrific work vertically. My father was blown into the air and landed on his head. He remembers his body "coming apart." Both of his legs and his left eye were gone. He lay in the snow in a daze, but still conscious. He was a mess.

As Dad was blown into the air, he reflexively prayed the Catholic Act of Contrition:

> *O my God, I am heartily sorry for having offended Thee, and I detest all my sins, because I dread the loss of heaven, and the pains of hell; but most of all because they offend Thee, my God, Who are all good and deserving of all my love. I firmly resolve, with the help of Thy grace, to confess my sins, to do penance, and to amend my life. Amen.*[86]

# 8
# SURVIVING

Having your legs blown off is what the Army calls "traumatic double amputation." During World War II, traumatic double amputation and the attendant shock killed soldiers at a high rate.[87] If shelling didn't blow an arm, leg, hand, or foot off, then mines were effective at doing the same thing, particularly in the lower extremities.

The immediate danger from traumatic amputation is blood loss: losing about one-fifth of the body's blood, or around three pints, leads to shock.[88] If the hemorrhaging of blood and fluids continues, the body's defenses will continue to crumble until the shock becomes irreversible. Then, you're dead. Even if the blood loss and shock caused by a double amputation did not kill you, a concussion from the mine blast could.

Dad suffered both. In short, the mine blast easily could have killed him. Under the circumstances, it should have. There were no helicopters or ambulances for rapid evacuation, and no means of quickly stabilizing the wounded. Instead, soldiers were down in the snow in a dense, dark forest; the only medic had been blinded by the blast, the Germans were potentially alerted and could lob in shells or rake the area with machine gun fire at any time, mines and booby traps were everywhere, and the only hope of survival rested on ill-trained, inexperienced soldiers.

After a traumatic double amputation and the resulting blood loss, hypovolemic shock can quickly set in when the heart is simply unable to pump enough blood to the body.[89] At that point, organs stop working. So the first step in treating a double amputation is to apply tourniquets to stop the hemorrhaging.[90] But my father didn't get them. Other steps are to raise the injured area, cover the person with a coat or blanket[91] and replenish fluids.[92] Those did not happen either. In short, none of the steps needed to immediately treat my father were taken.

The fact that Dad was still alive was likely because he was semiconscious or unconscious, and thus was not breathing heavily. The cold essentially clotted his blood loss.[93] Even so, his life was flickering.

My father's next memory was of being carried on a stretcher by rescuers who occasionally stopped for a break. He didn't remember receiving any treatment up to this point, with only the cold staunching further blood loss from his still open wounds. He'd been given up for dead. Only when he complained about a stretcher-bearer's coat slapping his face did the lead stretcher-bearer gasp in surprise, "My God, he's alive!" Then the stretcher-bearers began to move with urgency.

Dad soon found himself lying in a forward hospital in Eupen, Belgium, being stripped down and offered a glass of whiskey, a common pain reliever of that era. The Catholic chaplain offered to perform the sacrament of Last Rights. If the initially not-so-urgent actions of the stretcher-bearers hadn't already given him a clue, the Catholic chaplain's offer confirmed to Dad that his chances of survival weren't looking good. He took up the chaplain's offer, then asked for more whiskey.

How my father pulled through this I do not know. Given the state of medical technology in World War II, many in his condition did not.

After spending two or three nights in forward hospitals, Dad was taken by ambulance at night to the rear area. In the blacked out conditions, with vehicle lights dimmed to avoid detection near the front lines, the ambulance crashed into another vehicle in front of it, propelling Dad forward into the ambulance's cab. He was a double amputee and had lost an eye. Now he was in a vehicle crash. Surely, it couldn't get worse?

## 9

# THE CITY OF TERROR

MY FATHER'S DESTINATION WAS THE city of Liège, Belgium, a few dozen miles to the west of the front lines and situated on the bank of the River Meuse (or Maas in Flemish). The river forms a crevice between heights that rise approximately five hundred feet on both sides, and overlook the city below. In the late 19th century, Liège was a cultural center boasting an opera house, museums, and beautiful gardens on both sides of the river, which was spanned by arched bridges. It felt like a smaller version of Paris, particularly as French was the main language spoken there.

The name Liège comes from an old German word, which loosely translated means "people." Perhaps reflecting the lunacy of war, in the 20th century, the culture that so-named the city seemed utterly bent on its destruction.

In 1914, at the outbreak of World War I, Liège became the fulcrum of a massive assault by a German army numbering approximately 1.5 million, as it invaded France and Belgium.[94] A Belgian army garrison of approximately 25,000[95] managed to hold off the fierce assault for 12 days, until the Germans brought forward massive 24-foot-long siege mortars, each weighing 98 tons.[96] With these massive weapons, which could fire shells in an arc of approximately 4,000 feet high, taking 60 seconds to reach their target, the Germans pummeled Liège into submission.

Now, in 1944, Liège earned the unhappy sobriquet "Buzz Bomb City," as it was devastated by the new form of terror weapon, the V-1. In October of that year, the U.S. Army began establishing general hospitals in the city at whatever locations could be found, to stabilize soldiers wounded in the fighting about 30 miles eastward. Because it was a transportation hub, Liège seemed to make sense as a location for such facilities. However, the city's picturesque arched bridges across the Meuse had been destroyed by the war, replaced by temporary pontoon bridges.

At first, the ubiquitous V-1s generally passed overhead to terrorize cities farther west, such as Antwerp. On November 20, 1944, however, in what later became known as the first siege of Liège, the Germans launched a massive bombing assault on the city using V-1s. It was an attempt by an increasingly desperate enemy to sow terror. The German commander, Oberst Max Wachtel, instructed his V-1-firing troops to "provide relief to our army comrades who are involved in very fierce fights. I therefore demand non-stop firing from all technically serviceable sites against the enemy supply center at Liège."[97]

Sometimes the buzz bombs came fitfully. At other times, they seemed to come every 15 minutes.[98] One Army nurse recalled that as they commuted to work in the back of a truck across the pontoon bridges spanning the Meuse River, the driver would look for V-1s and then gun the engine to race across.[99] Another soldier who was in Liège during the siege later wrote:

> "Nothing was untouched—every aspect of life suffered. With great loss of life and untold human misery, civilian men, women, and children and Allied military personnel were caught in the city of terror. Civilian and army hospitals, stores, dwellings, telephone offices, theaters, and railroad yards all suffered direct hits. The V-1s, traveling at high speed and with terrifying noise, would suddenly, from a great height, cut off and dive into the city."[100]

As a city again under siege, by a remorseless and increasingly frantic enemy using terror weapons, Liège had, in effect, become an extension of the combat zone.

While the need to stabilize wounded soldiers near the front

was very real, the Army probably didn't take into account the use of terror weapons like the V-1. Transporting wounded soldiers to this veritable bull's-eye of a city seems, in retrospect, a colossal and deadly error. For the thousands of wounded soldiers lying immobilized in temporary quarters in Liège, there was no real warning or protection against these flying bombs, each of which was the equivalent of strapping a pair of wings onto a carload of explosives and tossing it at your enemy, not caring where it hit or who it killed. By one estimate, Liège was hit by more than a thousand flying bombs.[101] Such was the ferocity of the bombing that in one eight-day period between November 22 and 30, 1944, more than 330 V-1s impacted the vicinity of the Liège railway station alone.[102] The bombing became so terrifying that some soldiers in a Liège hospital asked to be returned to the front lines[103] rather than stay in what one called "the city of terror." Increasingly a vast pile of rubble, Liège seemed a city in name only.

My father arrived in this epicenter of the German's terror assault in the back of a truck, sometime on November 22 or 23, 1944, and was handed over to the care of the 15th General Hospital. This unit had established itself in a former Belgian military hospital, the Hospital Militaire, St. Laurent, situated on heights overlooking the city. The hospital itself consisted of two-story brick buildings with large-paned windows, arrayed symmetrically around a courtyard.[104] Like most places in Liège, the 15th General Hospital's quarters were vulnerable to the V-1s.

The V-1 was what the military calls a "fire and forget weapon." It was shaped like an oversized bullet, about 27 feet long with narrow rectangular wings protruding about seven feet on either side, and a pulsejet engine mounted on its tail.[105] The V-1 was fired from a rudimentary ramp and flew relatively unguided in the general direction of the enemy, until its fuel ran out. Because it had no real guidance system, the V-1 was most effective when fired against large Allied population centers. It was a terror weapon in its purest form, and one that today's veterans, who have endured the gauntlet of improvised explosive devices, rockets, and car bombs, would recognize.

The V-1's nickname, "buzz bomb," came from the loud, guttural roar emanating from its pulsejet engine, that could be heard from miles away. Dad heard many pass overhead while on the front lines. More than six decades later, I think its sound still resonated with him. Like other sounds, smells, feelings, and emotions that soldiers experienced in combat, they were indelible.

On November 24, 1944, the day after Thanksgiving, the Hospital St. Laurent, where my father was being treated, became the target of a V-1. For the second time in four days, he was struck by disaster. He never heard the bomb coming as it dove out of the sky.

A little after nine in the morning, the hospital was caring for approximately 1,190 patients.[106] My father was lying by himself, immobilized in a body cast. He had just been x-rayed in a nearby examination room. Then the V-1 hit. The impact on the hospital from its blast was shattering. It literally catapulted Dad into the air, body cast and all. As he fell back onto the bed, the ceiling collapsed on top of him. Shards of ceiling material sprayed everywhere, lacerating his face and hands. The concussive effect of the blast was so powerful, it detached the retina in his remaining eye, rendering him nearly blind.

A fire started among the chemicals stored in one of the hospital buildings. The roof crumpled in like a wadded piece of paper. Ambulances parked nearby were smashed and twisted by the force of the blast. Twenty-five people, including 16 soldiers, were killed, and many others were wounded, primarily by fragments of flying glass blown out of the large windows.

My father's next memory in the ensuing chaos was of a nurse yelling that she couldn't get him out, but that she would find help. Then he was lying in the slushy snow outside. He was bleeding profusely and couldn't see. In an amazing show of efficiency and composure, the nurse — or someone else — immediately hooked him up to a bottle of blood plasma. Without it, my father's blood loss would likely have killed him. He has no memory of who that nurse — or someone — was.

Dad was dazed, having suffered a concussion, and still in the full, albeit mangled body cast. Seeing my father, someone read his identification tags ("dog tags" in Army speak) identifying him as being Catholic. As he faded in and out of consciousness, his next memory was of a priest giving him Last Rights in French. Once more, my father was being written off as dead.

It is hard to know what was going through his mind at that point. Perhaps it was disbelief that all this could be happening, tinged with a bit of irony, fear, hopelessness, or some combination of all of these. My guess is that my father probably reacted to his circumstance with detached serenity. He is a man not given to showing his emotions. My mother always said he is someone who "lives inside his head," and I think that was probably true even when he was 19. Whatever the case, Private First Class Don Wedewer somehow survived.

---

By the end of the German's successive attacks on Liège using the flying bombs, 97 percent of the 82,700 dwellings in the city and surrounding province were damaged or destroyed, 96 soldiers were dead and another 336 wounded, and 1,158 civilians were dead.[107] As such, Liège was one of a long list of cities devastated by the war. Perhaps what distinguished Liège, though, were the incessant and concentrated attacks using new forms of terror weapons, and the fact that the city was largely defenseless against them. Traveling to Liège decades later, I could tell that the city had tried mightily to hide its scars. Virtually all of Liège appeared to have been reconstructed. While there, I had the sense that this rebuilt city was something of a Disneyesque production that was covering an unhappy past.

In the space of four days, my father survived a horrific experience in a minefield and an equally horrific experience in a terror attack during the siege of Liège. Both incidents should have killed him. Somehow, though, he came through. Now, it was time to go home and face the challenges of a dramatically altered life.

## 10

# HEADING HOME

AFTER THE HORRIFIC EXPERIENCE IN Liège, my father began his journey home through Paris and on to an Army hospital in Cambridge, England. The first part of the trip was by train and, as seemed the case more often than not, his transport through the Army medical system brought excitement all of its own. At one point, the rail car in which he and other wounded soldiers were laid out became detached from the rest of the train and was left coasting all by itself. It was effectively a runaway train. Indeed, for my father, the hits just kept on coming.

Dad's arrival in Cambridge marked his entry into the wartime Army hospital system and a long recovery. He once said that the real significance of his Army service was not his combat experience. Rather, it was his rehabilitation and recovery. I was surprised by the comment, but after considering that experience and its impact on his later life, I understood why. My father would eventually spend two years in the Army medical system in more than 15 hospitals and rehabilitation facilities. Along the way, he encountered stifling bureaucracy, outstanding medical care, gross medical incompetence, racism, religious extremism, extraordinary kindness, and romance. As a result, Dad did a lot of growing up in these hospitals.

His introduction to medical care in Cambridge began on a demoralizing note. Having been unable to brush his teeth for weeks because his teeth were blown inward by the detonation of the mine, my father asked a Red Cross nurse for a toothbrush. The response: "You have to pay." After he directed the nurse to his wallet, he was told that he had the wrong kind of money. He only had "Free French" money that the soldiers were forced to exchange once they arrived in Europe. The nurse insisted that he either pay in pounds sterling (English currency), or no toothbrush. The result: no toothbrush. Every time my father retold that story, he seemed more indignant, even decades later. This wouldn't be the last time my father encountered such insensitivity and health care incompetency.

His next stop was Glasgow, Scotland, where he was grouped with other wounded Americans before being sent back home. While there, he contracted jaundice, most likely due to receiving bad blood plasma. Also in Glasgow, he was infused with English blood, literally. In this case, the donor was a Royal Air Force pilot. Thus, Dad had the distinction of being of both German and English blood.

---

Following his stay in Glasgow, my father finally began the trans-Atlantic portion of his journey home. His plane was diverted to Paris because of bad weather, and while a stop in Paris might sound like a nice respite, his experience of the City of Lights was limited to the inside of an aircraft hangar while they waited for the weather to clear. Dad's only memorable Parisian experience was of an irate nurse who discovered that, rather than taking his sleeping pills, he'd been throwing them in a drawer because they made him nauseous. The nurse's anger was more about how she would look if her supervisor found out, rather than anything to do with how he might feel.

A week after he had been wounded, while in Paris, my father began the delicate process of informing his family of his wounds while keeping his emotions and gnawing uncertainty in check. "I am unable to tell you how seriously I am hurt or what is wrong with me. I am not able to write, so somebody is being kind enough to write this for me. I'll write and tell you about everything as soon as I can."

After inquiring about his brothers, my father closed forlornly, "Please write and tell the rest and tell them all to say an extra prayer for me."[108]

After four days in Paris, Dad was loaded back on to a C-54 transport plane for the trip home. Like other aircraft of that era, the C-54 was powered by large radial propeller engines that emitted a vibrating, guttural roar.[109] This made for a noisy ride akin to the most uncomfortable commuter plane rides of today.

First stop on his journey home was Lajes Field in the Azores Islands, for refueling. The Azores are a group of rocky islands located in the Atlantic Ocean almost 1,000 miles west of Portugal. Lajes Field itself is situated on a plateau. A high cliff in proximity to one end of the runway made it a potentially hazardous place for an aircraft to land,[110] particularly given the state of aviation technology in those days. In keeping with my father's run of luck, the young transport pilot overshot the runway on his first attempt at landing. On his second attempt, he bounced the plane down the runway before mercifully coming to a halt, much to the relief of Dad and the other patients. Fortunately, they changed pilots at Lajes.

## 11

# STATESIDE

AFTER THE AZORES STOP, MY father was transported to Bermuda and then General Mitchell Field on Long Island, New York. He arrived there on Christmas Eve, 1944. In keeping with the holiday season, a nurse brought him gifts donated by local civilians. The first one she opened for him was a pair of socks. The next was foot powder. With that, the sympathetic nurse abruptly ended Dad's Christmas 1944, at least with regard to gift giving.

In appearance, Dad was a very different person from the 19-year-old soldier who left the States two-and-a-half months earlier. He'd lost both legs, one above and one below the knee; he was missing an eye and could barely see out of the other one; his body still had pieces of shrapnel in it; he had a permanently bent finger, his teeth were bent, and he had suffered from jaundice and multiple concussions. In short, he was anything but the stereotypical strapping, returning war hero. And anyone who may have thought war was some glamorous adventure would have been immediately disabused of that notion on seeing him being carried off the plane.

What had *not* changed about my father, though, was his outlook and personality. These in turn would be the keys to his future.

Dad's short stay at Mitchell Field marked his entry into the wartime system of hospitals that served wounded veterans. In some respects the system resembled those in subsequent wars, including up to the present day, except on a more massive scale. In my father's case, his multiple wounds complicated his recovery. As a consequence, he would find himself on a two-year journey around the country.

From Mitchell Field, he was transported to Cleveland, Ohio,

for a brief evaluation stop at an Army hospital. While there, he was confronted with a situation that was part of his growing up, and in some ways maturing, in the Army hospitals. He befriended an Army Air Force mechanic by the name of Bob Kiesler. Bob had been a pre-med student at the University of Washington before being drafted into the Army Air Corps. In a freak accident, he was blinded while handling a mislabeled flare. Bob was certain his sight was coming back, though. He was sure of it.

While at Cleveland, however, a nurse approached my father and asked him to relay the news to Kiesler that he was not going to see again. It seemed a strange request—the nurse was trying to outsource the relaying of traumatic news, perhaps thinking that if it came from my father, who was barely able to see himself, it would somehow soften the blow. Dad could not do it, and refused.

After others told him he wasn't going to see again, Kiesler spiraled into depression—the first, but not the only time my father encountered this in hospitals. This sort of depression was not uncommon among traumatized war veterans who'd had debilitating, life-changing events thrust upon them at a young age, and who were vulnerable to being overwhelmed by those events. Unfortunately, the Army was not always prepared to help these young veterans at such a critical moment.

Dad later encountered Bob Kiesler at another hospital. He remembered him as the guy who wore cleats on his shoes, apparently as a means of warning others that he was approaching. By then, Kiesler had somewhat recovered from his depression.

After Cleveland, Dad was flown west, this time in a C-47 transport plane. The C-47 was a twin-engine, propeller-driven aircraft with a narrow tube-shaped cabin that measured approximately 40 feet long and 10 feet wide. In this tube, 14–16 patients were stacked on stretchers three-high.[111] There was barely enough room for a nurse to walk down a narrow aisle in between what was the equivalent of—and about as comfortable as—a rail freight car with wings and engines. In comparison, several C-47 cabins would fit inside the back of today's C-17 or C-5 aircraft used to transport the wounded and cargo back from the wars in Iraq and Afghanistan. The C-47 was also known as a "tail dragger," meaning that, like many aircraft of that era, it rested on its tail wheel while on the ground. Thus the front of the C-47 pointed upwards at an angle—an arrangement that was not always amenable to hard landings.

Shortly after heading west, my father again experienced the sometimes precarious nature of medical transport in that era. This time the C-47 he was being transported in broke a tail wheel upon landing in Chicago. Then, over New Years Eve 1944, his plane was diverted to Omaha, Nebraska, when one of its two engines failed. While staying in temporary quarters waiting for the weather to improve, the resourceful pilots managed to procure several six-packs of beer. They and their cargo of patients promptly got drunk.

The subsequent trip further west, though, was equally disjointed. After a refueling stop in Cheyenne, Wyoming, the on-board nurse realized she'd left the patients' medical records in Cheyenne. Much to the annoyance of the pilots, they turned the plane around to retrieve the records, and then flew back over the Rocky Mountains at night. This was apparently in violation of prevailing regulations against flying over the mountains at night with wounded soldiers on board. The conversation between the crew about breaking the rules occurred within earshot of my father, while he lay immobilized on his stretcher. This did nothing to improve his confidence in this mode of transport.

The final destination of Dad's rather hazard-strewn journey was Bushnell General Military Hospital in Brigham City, Utah, about an hour's drive north of Salt Lake City. After landing at Hill Army Airfield, he was transported to the hospital by truck. With his arrival at Bushnell, the itinerate phase of my father's hospital stays was at an end. No longer was he at a point where his wounds were being stabilized; it was now time to begin treatment. Things were about to become much more difficult.

## 12

# BUSHNELL

BUSHNELL GENERAL MILITARY HOSPITAL WAS one of 61 military hospitals in the United States during World War II, and the fifth largest on the mainland.[112] Its 60 buildings, about 40 of which were built from brick,[113] were situated on 235 acres at the southern edge of Brigham City.[114] Construction of the hospital was completed in an astonishing four months during 1942, in response to the rapidly growing number of war casualties. Bushnell was built on rolling, mostly treeless ground, with the picturesque Wasatch Mountains in the background. Aside from its areas of specialty care, Bushnell was designed to serve as a regional facility that allowed wounded soldiers from western mountain states to convalesce closer to their families.[115]

By 1944, Bushnell housed more than 3,200 patients,[116] who represented a microcosm of all the horrors that war could inflict on the vulnerable bodies, minds, and perhaps even souls of young Americans who probably had no real inkling that such a thing could happen to them. "It" was always going to happen to some other person, but not you. There were soldiers with malaria from the South Pacific; soldiers who were blinded; soldiers who had suffered severe burns and needed reconstructive surgery; soldiers suffering from rheumatic fever, gastrointestinal damage or allergies; soldiers suffering from the psychological effects of combat; and soldiers who, like my father, had lost limbs.

Bushnell's orthopedic department specialized in the care of amputees, and was one of five such centers throughout the country during the war. As was the case with recent wars, limb loss was a signature injury of World War II. And it was Bushnell's status as an orthopedic care center that brought my father there. The commander running Bushnell was the well-respected Colonel—later Brigadier General—Robert M. Hardaway. The head of orthopedics came from the same position at one of the major auto manufacturers. Having professionals of this caliber represented the contradiction in care that my father experienced repeatedly in Army hospitals. He encountered some of the finest medical professionals available who entered wartime service, while at the same time experiencing gross incompetence among others who treated him.

As was perhaps common of World War II Army hospitals, Bushnell consisted of a series of two-story, mostly brick buildings. At its center was an administration building connected to a series of covered walkways that spoked out to the patient dormitories. The idea was that patients and caregivers could travel between buildings in inclement weather, and stay dry.[117] Like other hospitals where my father received treatment, Bushnell was a small, self-contained city with its own dining facilities, movie theater, recreational facilities, post office, and more.[118] At the front of the hospital was a formal entrance and ceremonial flagpole that gained some notoriety later on. Dad's home at Bushnell was a 90-man ward—all amputees. As he once remarked, there were 90 patients on his ward and "not a leg among 'em."

For my father, philosophically, a wheelchair was not an option. So the first task facing him was to begin to learn to walk again. In those days, the science of prosthetics was still developing, and walking with prosthetic devices presented a considerable challenge with no assurance of a successful outcome.

Before Dad could walk again, his leg stubs had to be sufficiently healed and well formed to adapt to prosthetics. This meant removing old tissue and cutting away some of the remaining bone to smooth the end, while gathering scar tissue to heal in a tight seam. It was a process known euphemistically as "revising."

Leg amputees were categorized as "above the knees" (AKs), "below the knees" (BKs), and those, like my father, who had AK and BK amputations. He had to wait three to four months for revision surgery, because the operating rooms were backed up with the overflow of so many wounded.

Dad later recalled that the operating rooms "were going day and night" in beginning the process of reshaping or "revising" bodies that had lost limbs and other body parts. It was a grim reminder of the assembly line needed to care for the large number of soldiers arriving home every day from two theaters of war, missing arms, legs, hands, fingers, faces, feet, toes, testicles, and every possible combination of these. Such was the war.

---

Soon after his arrival at Bushnell, Dad received notice that he'd been awarded his first Purple Heart, the medal given to U.S. soldiers for being wounded in combat:

> GENERAL ORDERS
>
> NO ... 7 ) 11 January 1945.
>
> In accordance with authority delegated by the Secretary of War to the Commanding Officer of General Hospitals under the provisions of Paragraph 8, AR 600-45, the following named personnel are awarded the Purple Heart for wounds received as result of action against the enemy: ...
>
> DONALD H. WEDEWER, 37679214, Private First Class, 99th Infantry Division, for shell fragment wounds of the left eye and both legs while in direct contact with the enemy near Aachen, Germany, on 19 November 1944

The date on the citation was the date the fateful patrol had been supposed to take place, rather than the date on which it actually occurred, but it was close enough.

Brigham City was generally a welcoming place. The city leaders worked earnestly to get the Bushnell hospital constructed there, and once built, enthusiastically welcomed the wounded veterans who soon arrived by the thousands. Downtown Brigham City included a stereotypical main street U.S.A. full of two-story brick buildings housing businesses. A distinctive feature was a sign arching over the major thoroughfare proclaiming Brigham City to be the "Gateway to the World's Greatest Wild Bird Refuge." Occasionally, my father and the other double-amputee veterans went into Brigham City for dances, socials, sporting events, and more. On one of those soirees, one of his ward-mates had an apparently long night of carousing with a Bushnell nurse. The two decided to go a bit further—sex on someone's front lawn—until it was abruptly ended by a front porch lamp. Undeterred, the two made it back to Bushnell to pick-up where they left off. This time it was in front of the flagpole at the ceremonial entrance to the hospital. Amputee or not, this soldier's sex drive was apparently just fine.

---

As well as facing the long road back to walking again, my father was losing his sight. Something was wrong with his remaining eye, but he didn't know precisely what. After an evaluation by an ophthalmologist, he was told that everything was fine. Unfortunately, the ophthalmologist was wrong—badly wrong.

In retrospect, what most probably happened was that after the retina in Dad's remaining eye detached due to the blast from the V-1 in Liège, scar tissue built up in the back of that eye. (The retina forms a back layer of the eye upon which the images captured by the eye are printed, like old-fashioned film.) If diagnosed and treated early enough, a detached retina can be repaired. Left untreated, however, the chances of a successful repair are much diminished. The doctor's mistake in not diagnosing Dad early enough may ultimately have cost him his sight when it could have been saved. No one will ever know for sure.

Subsequently, while still at Bushnell, my father was examined by a specialist from the Dibble Army Hospital in California, a facility that specialized in eye treatment. The second ophthalmologist discovered that Dad had a detached retina and recognized the potentially serious consequences for his remaining vision. In Dad's presence, and in expletive-laced language, the specialist from Dibble castigated the first ophthalmologist over the seriousness of his misdiagnosis. Dad's confidence in the Army medical system continued to dissolve. His detached retina meant that treatment at Bushnell, and learning to walk again, would be delayed so that he could receive specialized treatment for his remaining eye at the Dibble Hospital. On balance, it was sight taking priority over learning to walk.

While at Bushnell, my father again encountered racism—as odious in Utah as it was elsewhere during the war. One of his ward-mates was an African-American soldier from Chicago who had lost both legs while in a tank overseas. His wife visited every day. However, under local law, African-Americans were forbidden to spend the night in Brigham City. This meant she had to take the bus out of town every night to an African-American community miles away, no matter how badly wounded her husband was, or how much he had sacrificed for the nation.

That this could happen was reflective of the stark contradiction in Brigham City itself. It was the kind of place where disabled veterans were embraced—but only, of course, if they were white. Indeed, veterans were routinely welcomed into locals' homes, and any amputee who was able to walk on their prosthetics into the Idle Isle, a popular restaurant, received a free steak dinner.[119] Disabled veterans were hosted at countless social events, could walk into a local bakery and get free donuts,[120] and were featured in local parades. But in spite all of the caring, sensitive things that Brigham City did for veterans, it could not, as was the case in many parts of America in 1945, get past racial prejudice, and treated African-American veterans and their families differently.

Objections by my father and other disabled soldiers to the discriminatory practice of forcing African-American hospital visitors to leave town at night, were ignored by Bushnell hospital staff. According to those staff members, that was just the way it was.

## 13

# TO THE WEST COAST

Dibble Army Hospital in Menlo Park, California, was in a pleasant location in the San Francisco Bay area. It was situated on a former large estate that today is occupied by scientific research facilities, originally associated with nearby Stanford University. The hospital included long, single-story wooden buildings with screen porches and outdoor areas for sunning.

Dad was treated at Dibble on two separate occasions. The first was for surgery on his concussion-damaged retina, in the hope of improving at least some of his remaining sight. The surgery was successful, albeit temporarily. However, by today's standards it was relatively crude and uncomfortable. During his recovery, Dad had to lay on his back for a week, motionless, with his head sandwiched between sandbags. This meant eating, urinating, and defecating while confined in a veritable straight jacket. It is hard to imagine the physical discomfort and psychological impact on my father. At age 20, he couldn't know whether he would walk or see again — a circumstance compounded by having to sit and wait ... and wait ... and sit some more. In his standard matter-of-fact way, he would just say that he endured it.

Fortunately, Dad had many visitors at Dibble, ranging from the owner of the San Francisco Forty-Niners professional football team to locals doing what they could to support the wounded veterans. During this time, my father was also featured in a nationally syndicated newspaper column, "Purple Heart Diary." Written by the entertainer and film star Frances Langford, the column featured the stories of young, wounded veterans and gave my father the opportunity to meet Langford. Before doing so, he met Langford's agent, an unattractive guy who oozed sleaziness. As Dad recalled, the agent told him he "had slept with Langford." It seemed odd that the agent would tell a severely wounded young veteran of this sexual exploit, real or imagined. In any case, Dad was unimpressed. He had his brief meeting with Langford, and was on his way. Subsequently, a fastidious hospital public affairs officer at Dibble provided further background regarding my father. Soon his story was featured nationally through the Purple Heart column—fame that would later follow him east.

As well as the treatments and publicity Dad received at Dibble, he also had a love life of sorts there. He was fixed up with a Minnesotan who was soon sending signals that she was ready to get married. As Dad recalled, on one of their walks, she pointed out a house that would be "nice to settle down in." He was in no rush to do so, and in his indirect, understated way probably avoided the question by changing the subject. During his hospital stays, he would have other such offers. Conventional wisdom would say there would be little romantic interest in a young, badly wounded veteran, but my father did not find that to be the case.

---

Around this time, in mid-May 1945, Dad received a letter from "Cut" Cunningham, his former platoon sergeant, updating him on how First Platoon, F Company, came through the recently ended war in Europe. It was likely the first communication my father had had with his unit since being wounded. The letter was dated May 7, 1945, the day German surrendered, and noted, "(still in Germany)."[121] Although containing some perhaps expected jocularity, for example, asking about the nurse who had written a letter for my father, ("Is she young, ha, ha"), the news was not all good.[122] First Platoon, F Company, came through, according to Cut, largely because of Lieutenant—now Captain—Goodner.[123] But it had been bloody. Soldiers that Dad had known—Harrell Chambliss from Texas, Norman Venter from Colorado, and Klewing—along with others he hadn't known, were dead.[124] Cut continued, "Hubbard was froze up in an attack in the snow on our first offensive."[125] Hubbard was not seen again. Harper from Missouri had been wounded — cut down by German 88 cannon fire while crossing the Rhine River in Germany.

Harper was lucky. According to Cut, 17 men, almost half of First Platoon's 40 soldiers, had been killed in the Rhine River crossing alone.[126] It happened on April 9, 1945, less than a month before Germany surrendered. In mentioning the number not once but twice, Cut still seemed to be processing it: "crossing the rhine [sic] where I lost 17 men, sure a tough break."[127] It wasn't some higher-up who lost these guys; it wasn't some incompetent general, or some kiss-ass general-wanna-be colonel; it wasn't some newly self-important major, some clueless captain, or even some I-don't-have-a-clue dumb-ass lieutenant, who lost 17 men. It was: "I lost 17 men." It was as if Cut was saying, "Forget about anybody else in the chain of command, if only I had done something different so close to the end of this goddammed war, those men would still be here."

That was Cut. He was a helluva soldier. Despite being nominated for Officer Candidate School, and the fact that he would no doubt have made a great officer, Cut would never get there because of his color blindness. Cut's letter to my father was the last time the two would communicate for almost 45 years.[128]

---

Although Dibble was generally well run, the facility was not entirely free of the bureaucratic indignities that tinged my father's hospital stays. In this case, it was the fixation of an Army lieutenant on preserving the paint job on the hospital walls. The lieutenant did not like the fact that the blinded vets were marking the hospital walls with their canes. This resulted from the vets' use of the "tapping" technique as they swung their long canes in front of them to sense any obstructions in their path. Consequently, the lieutenant issued an edict to curtail the tapping. How he expected the blinded vets to get around is something of a mystery. Presumably, it was okay if they just crashed in to somebody or something.

Word of the lieutenant's problem with the marked-up walls soon got out. What the lieutenant probably did not appreciate was that, in his efforts to rid the walls of scuffmarks, he was dealing with a formidable foe in these young veterans. Many, such as my father, were still in their teens or early twenties and had done a lot of growing up in a short time. They had the attitude to match. And they were not going to put up with a lot of crap from a self-important lieutenant. After all, these were the same types as the soldiers in the 99th who booed their commanding general.

In any case, as a result of the wall-tapping episode, a Congressional investigation ensued at Dibble. Not surprisingly, Lieutenant "Don't Mark My Walls" was "made to disappear." Apparently, no one was willing to defend the proposition that marked walls were a threat to good order and discipline.

Another instance of morale-killing focus on minutiae occurred during my father's stay in Dibble's one-eye ward. He'd been put here because he still had limited, although fading, vision in one eye. In spite of this partial sight, he was still accorded the relative luxury of having a talking book machine, essentially an old-fashioned record player for listening to books recorded on vinyl. When one of the attending nurses learned of this, she wanted my father moved to a ward for soldiers who had lost their sight entirely. His response: "No." To which the nurse responded with words to the effect of okay, we are going to take your record player away since you are not really totally blind. Dad appealed to the ophthalmologist, who sided with my father. Round two to Dad. This was another example of one of those senseless edicts from hospital staff that fortunately were the exception rather than the norm.

Dad later took some vicarious pleasure in the fact that the record-player-stealing nurse got what she deserved in the form of a devious boyfriend. Like my father, the boyfriend was a patient at Dibble receiving treatment for vision loss. One evening, as they were boarding the bus for San Francisco, Dad witnessed his fellow patient bounding off the bus to retrieve a forgotten wallet. Given the dexterity with which the supposedly visually impaired guy raced off the bus and up a flight of stairs, Dad thought he was a "faker," cheating the system to accrue the extra benefits he would be due if diagnosed as being blind. What a perfect match, Dad thought: insensitive record-player-stealing nurse, and faker, gaming-the-system boyfriend.

---

On the front page of the July 22, 1945, edition of the Dubuque, Iowa *The Telegraph-Herald*, a picture of Private First Class Wedewer appeared with an article captioned, "Education Goal of Local Boy, Young Wedewer Who Lost Legs, Eye, Has Courage."[129] After recounting his list of injuries, the article noted, "Some boys in Wedewer's boat might feel sorry for themselves, might think there wasn't much use planning for a future—but not this young veteran."[130]

Newspaper articles of the day generally referred to wounded veterans as "boys," a reference which in retrospect seems odd, given what these "boys" went through. But what the article did get right about my father was its use of the word "courage" in the title, in recognition of the fact that a soldier's courage did not stop on the battlefield. It would be tested again off the battlefield, as soldiers like my father dealt with the physical and emotional toll of the war while facing the future.

My father's courage was going to be tested again as his recovery entered its next phase, which involved learning to walk again while his vision remained marginal at best. Fortunately, he was about to encounter a man and a woman who, in different contexts, embodied the kind of courage needed to face the future in spite of physical handicaps. They would recognize it in my father as a resource to be tapped and encouraged to keep him moving ahead.

Dad as an Army Private with his brother James (1944).
*Photo courtesy of Nancy and Bill Feld*

Camp Wolters, Texas (circa 1940s)
*Photo courtesy of Brian Bagnall*

Damage from the V-1 attack on the 15th General Hospital, Liège, Belgium (1944).
*Photo courtesy of the National Library of Medicine*

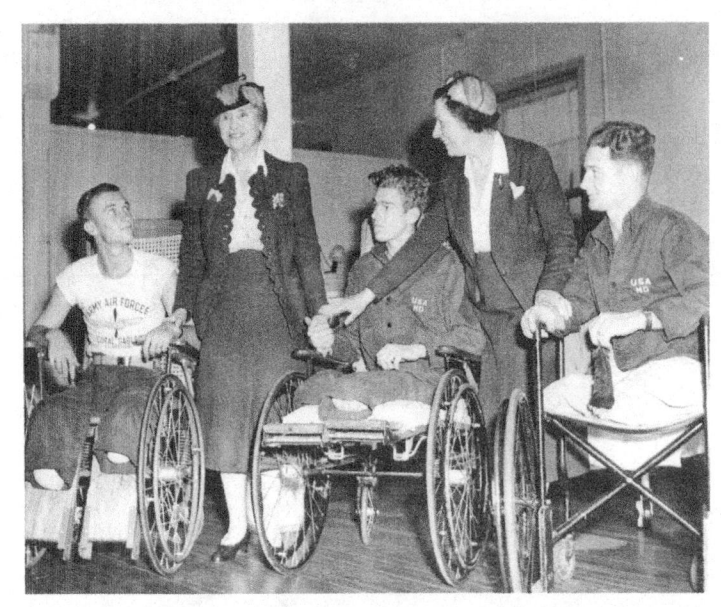

Helen Keller (standing left) visiting American service-members during World War II.
*Photo courtesy of the American Foundation for the Blind*

Mom and Dad with their young family in South Florida, which would eventually number five children (early 1950s).
*Photo courtesy of Nancy and Bill Feld*

Dad speaking at the Conklin Center for the blind in Daytona Beach, Florida, which he helped co-found with Millard Conklin to serve the needs of those who are multi-handicapped.
*Photo courtesy of the Conklin Center*

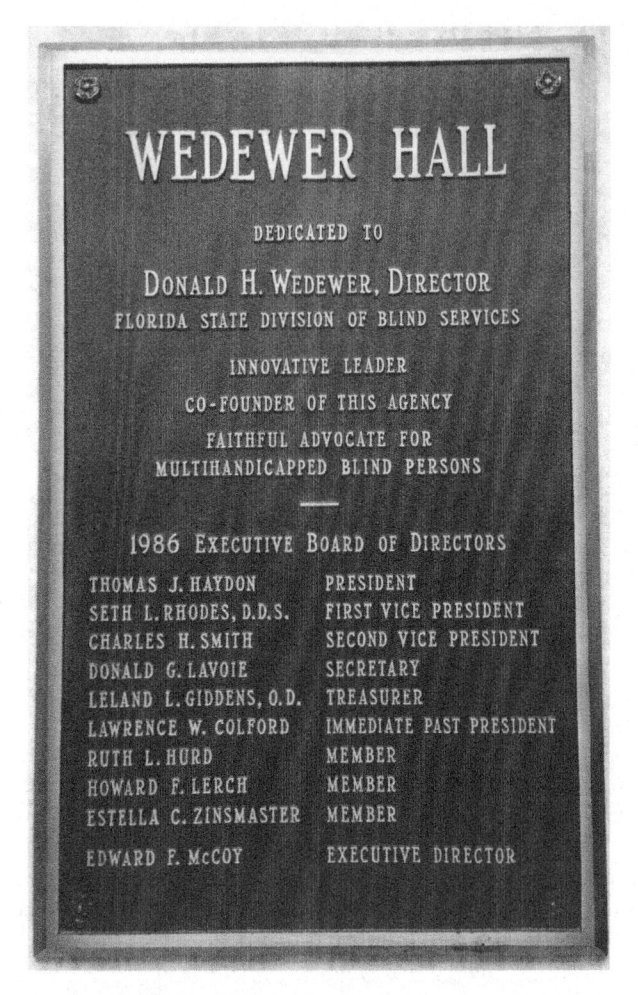

Plaque marking Wedewer Hall at the Conklin Center dedicated in 1986.
*Photo courtesy of the Conklin Center*

Dad receiving an award from the National Accreditation Council in recognition that his agency was the leading such organization in the country for serving those with vision loss. He later received a congratulatory letter from President Ronald Reagan marking this achievement (1987).

Mom and Dad at the ceremony marking Dad's receipt of the Migel Medal, the American Foundation for the Blind's highest award (1990).

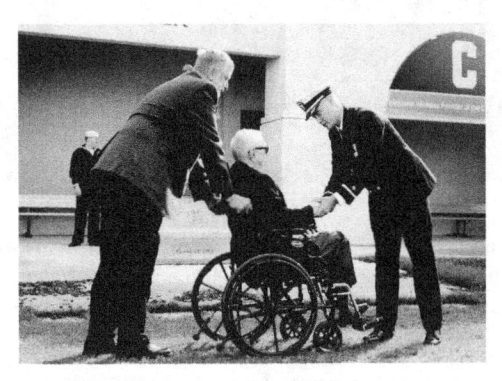

A soldier's last duty: Dad receiving the traditional silver dollar from his grandson Ben after being the first to salute the latter at his commissioning ceremony as a U.S. Navy Ensign (2012).

## 14

# WALKING

After his eye surgery and recovery at Dibble, my father was sent back to Bushnell General Military Hospital in Utah. Now began another hard part of his recovery and rehabilitation—the previously interrupted process of learning to walk. Fortunately for him, many of the other young veterans at the sprawling hospital were also double amputees. As Dad recalled, having your contemporaries cheer you along—or jeer you if you needed it—was one of the keys, if not *the* key, to success in walking again. In this case, peer pressure was a positive influence that served to push him and the other wounded veterans harder. The fact that everyone was facing the same challenges seemed to limit the opportunity for wounded soldiers like my father to engage in unproductive introspection, wondering why they were dealt such a lousy hand of cards. In short, the war was shitty not just for you, but also for everyone around you.

During this phase of his recovery and rehabilitation, Dad benefited from the advances made in prosthetic technology during World War II. Of particular importance was the use of plastics in prosthetics and the associated sockets, that made them significantly lighter and easier to manipulate.[131] Plastic also mitigated the severe blisters associated with the metal parts in earlier prosthetics.[132] The relative lightness of plastic prosthetics had the salutary effect of changing the previous medically held view that amputees should remain sedentary.[133] This was critical for my father, who was determined to walk. Fortunately for him, Bushnell was also pioneering in its use of the drug penicillin for treating infections.[134] Prior to this breakthrough, the standard treatment for deep tissue and bone infections had been to use maggots to eat the diseased flesh around a bone[135] — a prospect Dad was fortunate enough to avoid.

In learning to walk again, my father's below-the-knee (BK) right leg was the easier part of rehab, because he still had use of his natural knee. This made using the prosthetic on that leg simpler. For his initial therapy, which lasted a few weeks, Dad performed exercises with straps while in bed, along with stretching exercises to straighten out his remaining knee before a prosthetic could be fitted. As a form of weight training, nurses would at times lie on their backs across his legs while he tried to lift them.

Another consideration was not allowing the bottom portion of the leg stumps to become too "fleshy," as blood and other unused tissue tended to collect here, making it difficult to fit the prosthetics properly. To prevent this, the stumps were wrapped with compression bandages to maintain constant pressure before prosthetics could be fitted. On his right, BK leg, my father had a leather cup and wooden prosthetic fitted. He was able to accommodate these with relative ease, even though adjustments were made over time to prevent sores.

His left, AK leg, was a different matter. As Dad described it, there was a world of difference between the AK and BK, because learning to work with a mechanical knee on the AK was tricky. The key to the mechanical knee was to be able to achieve 180 degrees of rotation, thereby allowing full travel of the artificial leg. The patient also had to learn how to gain full extension before placing weight on the knee, all while balancing with a cane. If you didn't get it quite right, down you went.

Therapy initially consisted of walking between two wooden rails on what looked like an elongated treadmill. There was a full-length mirror at the far end to help the amputees synchronize their steps. On the rails, my father's very limited eyesight presented an extra challenge. The mirror was of little use to him, and he had to develop an innate sense of the proper movement of the legs and eventual coordination with a cane. Every day for about two weeks, it was the same: up in the morning and on the rails. The therapy was akin to starting with training wheels while learning to ride a bike. From the rails, my father graduated to the use of a cane that took pressure off the AK leg as he walked and tried to synchronize the movements of his legs.

Next came the challenge of walking up and down steps. Not surprisingly, falls and a fear of falling were the hardest parts. Dad remembered adjusting reasonably well and, while he had some falls, he recalls only one as being serious.

When asked what got him through the daunting task of learning to walk again, my father's response was simple: "Harassment." Harassment, as well as encouragement, from his fellow double amputees at Bushnell was vital to my father. This encouragement was assisted by the construct of the surroundings in which therapy was conducted: in a large open space, in full view of other amputees learning to walk again. Thus, your progress, or lack thereof, was in full view of the other soldiers. Whether by design or luck, in such an environment, peer pressure, and perhaps competition, worked wonders.

Something seemingly visceral was also perhaps motivating the amputees during their recovery—the feeling that if you did not recover, then the asshole who planted the mine that blew you up had won. Or, the chain of assholes who helped him get it there had won. That was not going to happen.

The other motivating factor was the feeling of not wanting to be pitied. To wounded veterans, being pitied was perhaps as bad as having their service under-appreciated. They hated that.

In this sense, there was a fine line between appreciating and understanding a veteran's service, and pitying them as victims. An employer who appreciated a veteran's service might hire that person because they figured someone who'd had hand grenades tossed at them, or who'd walked through minefields, could probably deal with the challenges that might be tossed their way on the job. That was okay. What was not okay was hiring veterans because you felt sorry for them. They didn't need anyone feeling sorry for them, thank you very much.

For one of my father's contemporaries, this sense of being pitied was reinforced by the presence of his mother, who was constantly at Bushnell to monitor his progress in rehabilitation. She apparently crossed the line between support and pity. The soldier felt this was not an environment for his doting mom, however well intentioned, and sent her home.

As challenging as things were for my father, it was even harder for those with two AK amputations to learn to walk on prosthetics. Dad recalled in particular one AK soldier who was struggling to overcome his fear of falls. After being encouraged by my father and his fellow vets, he walked.

Not everyone learned to walk again, though. One guy, for example, drank too much beer and gained too much weight to overcome his condition. But for my father, a combination of encouragement from others and his persistence and plain hard-headedness made sure that wouldn't happen. In short, he benefitted from the outlook of a 20-year-old — confident, and impervious to the challenges ahead of him.

In later years, I always marveled at how well he was able to move around. Even as a young boy with relatively little strength, I could guide him along with my right arm, which served more to assist in steering him than to help him keep his balance. His synchronization of his leg and cane movements always seemed perfect, as if he had been doing it his entire life.

The thing about my father and his wounds and resulting handicaps was not what they did to him, rather, it was about what he would *not allow* them to do. In this case, his wounds were not going to prevent him from walking again. In later years, this outlook translated into my father's description of himself as someone with handicaps, rather than a handicapped person. There was a difference. In Dad's view, the first was a fully capable person who had certain conditions to overcome, while the second was someone not fully capable because of their limited ability to do certain things.

One side effect of my father's recovery and rehabilitation was that, over time, he transformed from a skinny teenager into a man with fairly well-developed arm and shoulder muscles, as a result of repetitive, seemingly mundane tasks such as getting in and out of bed.

Dad and the other double amputees benefitted from two other motivating influences. One was Joe Miller, a non-veteran double amputee from Montana who lost his legs at the age of 12 in a railroad accident.[136] When the United States entered the war, Joe petitioned President Franklin D. Roosevelt "requesting a chance to help the fellows out [who were] coming back from overseas."[137] What he and the other amputees likely did not know, was that their Commander-in-Chief, President Roosevelt, was a kindred spirit—someone who also had to walk with artificial support. In Roosevelt's case, the fact that he walked with braces after a bout with polio as a young man had largely been hidden from public view. At the president's request, the press had generally not published photographs of him walking with braces or in a wheelchair. One notable exception was when he visited a ward full of wounded veterans in 1944. On this occasion, Roosevelt purposely wheeled himself around in a wheelchair and allowed himself to be photographed.[138] His message to the wounded veterans was clear: you still have limitless opportunities. To society as a whole, Roosevelt's message was, accept the veterans as they are, without the baggage of pre-conceived notions of what they are capable of.

The letter Joe Miller wrote to the president eventually made its way to the Bushnell Hospital administrators, and Colonel Hardaway found a position for him teaching the wounded soldiers how to use their artificial limbs. With what my father described as "the very little of his legs that remained," Joe was able to move around with the best of them. He drove a car, routinely strolled around town, and enjoyed fishing as a hobby.[139] Joe was particularly successful in teaching soldiers how to go up and down stairs, which he did on his leg stubs alone. Joe also helped the amputees learn how to walk in snow, and he worked in the hospital brace shop, assisting the technicians in making artificial limbs.[140]

In short, Joe Miller was a terrific example of everything that was possible. And, aside from his demonstrative skills, Joe had a sunny, positive outlook that made him a terrific coach and mentor. Indeed, Joe Miller was an icon of sorts at Bushnell, and was featured in a period video filmed at the hospital, extolling the benefits of hiring soldiers with handicaps.

What perhaps made Joe Miller such a great example was that he exemplified a quality my father could identify with: persistence. Here was a person who motored around as a double amputee with better agility than most, whether they wore prosthetics or not. And Joe did so in an era when people with handicaps were not generally accommodated. A person who wrote to the President offering his services—*that was persistence*. Joe's example was simple, "If I can do it, why can't you?"

Joe also took an interest in my father, perhaps because he sensed Dad was demonstrating, and would need to continue to demonstrate, the same, uncompromising persistence. Joe's interest would prove to be important, if not vital.

The second motivating force in my father's learning to walk again was the bond he formed with his fellow double amputees. It was hard not to, even if it was for no other reason than proximity. During his stay at Bushnell, Dad and the other double amputees lived together in 90-man wards. Their shared experience became a glue of sorts, and in time they formed the Bilateral Amputee Club of America, Inc. or BLACA.[141] BLACA became a support system for soldiers like my father, who had little contact with their families.

The club began with an ambitious agenda: inviting President Harry Truman to their inaugural dinner (he didn't attend).[142] Even with the presidential no-show, the formation of BLACA and my father's membership came at an important time for him, because the group provided the sort of support that only peers could. For Dad, whose father was dead, his stepmother pretty much out if his life, and his five brothers spread throughout the world, BLACA filled a void. His BLACA peers shared an evident optimism and sense of looking forward that was a great tonic for my father. These were not veterans focused on their disabilities. Rather, these were veterans focused on their *abilities* and the future.

My father's generation has been called the "Greatest Generation." I think people such as Joe Miller and my father's fellow club members in BLACA were emblematic of that. They were a group of individuals with life-changing wounds who kept their heads up, acted selflessly, and were cheerfully, mutually supportive throughout what could have been a very difficult time. An August 1945 newspaper article about BLACA, entitled "Both Legs Off, Yes; But Crippled? No!" reported: "Regardless of whether they were in wheelchairs or on legs they could barely manage, the BLACA members showed a degree of enthusiasm which few civilians could equal."[143] Similarly, a 1946 picture in the Ogden, Utah *Standard-Examiner*, showing my father and other BLACA members, trumpeted the group's existence as backers of a "Forget-me-not Drive" to raise money for the club's activities.[144]

Many of these soldiers went on to successful careers. There was Jensen from Idaho, who went on to become a lawyer; Spurgeon, who became a doctor in Missouri. Another became a dentist. In short, it was a group looking ahead and not down—or backwards. Even though it wasn't able to attract the president's attention, BLACA did receive a visit from the movie star Shirley Temple, who later provided some of its members with a tour of Hollywood. And the hospital commander, Colonel Hardaway, was so impressed with the club that he offered the use of a plane to visit other hospitals to promote the formation of similar groups.

---

Dad wasn't able to take part in the BLACA visits to other hospitals, but he was part of a tour to sell war bonds. These provided a way for ordinary people to invest in the war effort by in effect loaning the government their money. (This would be akin to buying a stake in the funding that supported the recent wars in Afghanistan and Iraq, in addition to what you were already paying in taxes.) Such was the intensity of feeling during World War II, that millions of Americans invested in these bonds. Veterans such as my father were an integral part of the war bond effort, making publicity tours to promote their sale. It was perhaps symbolic of a time when veterans were more a part of our national consciousness. This was to some extent due, no doubt, to their sheer numbers. Likewise, there seemed to be no reluctance on the part of my father and the other veterans to participate in such a tour, even though it may have invoked memories of the killing, maiming, destruction and litany of other horrors associated with the war. The perceived righteousness of the war effort and national support for it seemed to place all of that in context. Hence, a bond tour was just one more act of service in support of a national cause.

For my father's tour, he, along with other wounded veterans, traveled around Utah with the governor's wife, speaking to public audiences. One of these veterans, also a Bushnell patient, was Sergeant Silvestre Herrera, Company E, 142nd Infantry, 36th Infantry Division. Silvestre Herrera's courage and demeanor exemplified the kind of soldier my father met while at Bushnell.

Herrera was born in Mexico and grew-up in El Paso, Texas, where he worked as a farm hand before moving with his wife and three children to Arizona.[145] Herrera was drafted into the U.S. Army in 1944. Although technically a Mexican national and not required to serve, Herrera nonetheless entered the service of his adopted country, and studied to become an American citizen.[146] Subsequently, Herrera was sent to the European theater, landing in southern France. On March 15, 1945, Herrera's platoon was advancing when it ran into two German machine gun emplacements.[147] Caught in the crossfire from the two guns, Herrera jumped up and ran toward the Germans, firing his rifle from his hip and tossing grenades.[148] That was enough to daze the Germans, eight of whom threw down their weapons and surrendered to Herrera.[149] Herrera then single-handedly charged the other German machine gun, which he knew was protected by a minefield.[150] Herrera stepped on one of the mines and, despite having both feet blown off, continued to provide covering fire while the other soldiers circled from behind and destroyed the position.[151]

Even with such extraordinary heroism, Dad recalled Herrera as an understated, quiet person who focused only on the fact that he was reacting to the situation and doing his duty. *It was no big deal.* That sort of quiet dignity is what the wounded veterans at Bushnell, including my father, were all about.

---

Dad's progress in learning to walk again during his second stay at Bushnell was counterbalanced by deterioration in his eyesight. Once again, the limited vision in his one good eye started to fade. In spite of his constant complaints, the doctors told him that all appeared fine. Of course, he knew better.

It got to the point where the Army was ready to discharge him. After all, he could walk and his eyesight was ... well, okay. An Army Major placed discharge papers in front of him to sign, but my father refused. He knew that once he was discharged from the Army medical system, he was on his own. Besides, he knew his vision was deteriorating. Consequently, he kept up his campaign to have something done about it.

Around this time, Bushnell's amputee trainer, Joe Miller, perhaps sensing my father's predicament and increasing gloom, wrote to a lawyer friend by the name of Keenan in Ames, Iowa. The correspondence gave my father such encouragement that he was able to clearly recall it some 60 years later. In his letter, Miller called Dad "the bravest guy I have ever seen." It was no small compliment, given Joe Miller's stature in the Bushnell community. Joe, perhaps as much as anyone, recognized my father's twin struggles of learning to walk and hardly being able to see. Dad soon received an encouraging letter from Joe's lawyer friend, in which he repeated Joe Miller's statement. The compliment probably meant more to my father than any medal. Through his example and this simple act of kindness, Joe Miller gave my father the best medicine there was: hope.

He needed it. Around this time, Dad sank to an emotional low point. It was probably the closest he ever came to irrecoverable despair. Faced with fading vision, doubts about his future ability to walk, and a bureaucracy that was either unable or unwilling to further help him, he was at risk of spiraling into depression.

Up to this time, Dad had been able to cope with whatever

psychological effects his wounds may have had on him. They were what they were, and he was not a person to dwell on his circumstances. But now, with what seemed like a white sheet gradually enveloping the vision in his one good eye, and with the Army essentially telling him that it was done with him, everything seemed to crowd in all at once. In short, at 21 his future seemed bleak and hopeless.

Fortunately, providence again intervened on my father's side in the form of a nurse. Sensing Dad's gloom, the nurse took him outside to a baseball game. Anything to get his mind off his troubles. My father didn't recall all the details, but the simple act of going outside, and the opportunity, however short, to focus on something other than his circumstances, pulled him back from the brink. Like the earlier intervention by the nurse who pulled him from the rubble of a bombing, this intervention, by another nurse, also at a critical moment, made perhaps a life-saving difference for my father.

---

A photo of my father taken while he was at Bushnell seems to summarize his experience there. Dressed in dark hospital pajamas, looking not more than 16 years old, his left eye gone, an empty, disfiguring black slit in its place, and wearing newly fitted prosthetics on the remainder of his legs, Dad is nonetheless beaming with a broad, jaunty smile as he hoists himself out of a wheelchair to stand. "I am not standing by any chances" he assures the viewer on the back of the photo. Indeed he was not. Neither the Nazis, the mines, the booby traps, the V-1s, the bureaucracy, the incompetent medical care nor his fading vision — none of that was going to keep the irrepressible optimist, Don Wedewer, down. By any standard, my father should not have been smiling. But here he was, still beaming.

## 15

# THE WARRIOR

WITH HIS INSISTENCE THAT SOMETHING was still wrong with his remaining eye and his refusal to accept a discharge, my father won a victory of sorts. He was sent back to Dibble Army Hospital for reexamination. The initial diagnosis was that there was nothing wrong with his remaining vision. However, after more objections from my father, the examining physician agreed to allow him to go home to Iowa for Christmas, and then return for another examination to determine whether anything was wrong.

There was. After Dad's return, the staff at Dibble examined him again and found a cataract in his remaining eye. This was removed, and his vision somewhat restored.

Losing his legs was one thing, but far more worrisome for my father was the possibility that he might completely lose his vision. At this point, his remaining vision was completely reliant on a tenuously connected, war-detached and then repaired retina in his one functioning eye. The Army could give him prosthetic legs to enable him to walk again, but it was not going to give him a new eye. Life without vision would be a wholly different matter.

During one of his treatments at Dibble, Dad was visited by Helen Keller. It was one of those encounters in life that, while brief, made an indelible impression. Keller was an internationally known, iconic figure in the rehabilitation of the blind and deaf. She had become blind and deaf when only 19 months old, yet, with the aid of a teacher, learned to speak, read, and write.[152] Keller achieved much at a time when women were not expected to gain prominence, and rarely went to college. She was deaf at a time when the deaf were rarely able to break through the silence, and she was without vision at a time when those who were sightless were rarely able to pierce the darkness.

Yet, in the year 1900, at age 20, Keller entered Radcliffe College. Four years later, after having lectures and textbooks spelled to her letter by letter,[153] Keller graduated with honors as the first deaf and blind person ever to be awarded a bachelor's degree.[154] Subsequently, she became an internationally known advocate and author in support of the blind and deaf-blind, as an ambassador for the American Foundation for the Blind, which had been created after World War I to help support the large number of veterans blinded in that war by horrific gas attacks.

Such was Keller's stature that she was invited by General Douglas MacArthur to travel to Japan after World War II, to serve as a goodwill ambassador in building a relationship with the Japanese blind and deaf-blind. For her accomplishments, Keller was eventually awarded the Presidential Medal of Freedom and was the subject of a Hollywood feature film.

In addition to her advocacy on behalf of the blind and deaf-blind, Keller was a strong advocate for women's rights and other social causes. Such advocacy, like Keller's other efforts, gained her international fame. But between the World Wars, it also earned her the enmity of German Nazi youth groups who, in the 1930s, burned some of her writings as being subversive. With characteristic forthrightness, Keller responded in May 1933 with a letter that was both courageous and remarkably prescient:

> *To the Student Body of Germany:*
>
> *History has taught you nothing if you think you can kill ideas. Tyrants have tried to do that often before, and the ideas have risen up in their might and destroyed them. You can burn my books and the books of the best minds in Europe but the ideas in them have seeped through a million channels, and will continue to quicken other minds. I gave all the royalties of my books to the soldiers blinded in the World War with no thought in my heart*

> *but love and compassion for the German people. Do not imagine your barbarities to the Jews are unknown here. God sleepeth not, and He will visit His Judgment upon you. Better were it for you to have a millstone hung round your neck and sink into the sea than to be hated and despised of all men. Helen Keller*[155]

As one Keller scholar wrote, "Helen was a warrior who never ceased throughout her life to demand that women, the poor and disenfranchised be afforded an equal chance to live a full life."[156] To borrow from the title of a popular book of today, *Lean In: Women, Work, and the Will to Lead*,[157] Helen Keller was "leaning in" in an era where few women had the opportunity to do so, while smashing through not just one glass ceiling, but several layers of ceilings.

Keller became aware of my father's condition, and a meeting was arranged. The two met for about 45 minutes while they walked accompanied by Keller's secretary. Keller placed her hand on Dad's lips as a means of reading what he was saying, and had her secretary write in her hand. (As a young child, Keller learned through this method to say one of her first sentences: "I am not dumb now."[158]) Their conversation was varied, and topics included Iowa, books, and his treatment. Dad was impressed by how well-read and informed Keller was. Perhaps more importantly, he was impressed by what she represented: a person with multiple handicaps who, despite unimaginable obstacles, accomplished so much for an overlooked and underserved group of Americans.

It was perhaps hard to imagine at the time of their meeting that Keller's and Dad's paths would cross again, with him facing an uncertain future in a society that seemed to erect artificial barriers, rather than offer hope, to those with handicaps. But their paths would cross again. Dad would undertake his own journey to "I can do this," and would ultimately have a transformative impact on others. While his meeting with Keller was relatively short, the encounter provided him with an indelible picture of what was possible for the future. By nature, my father was always an optimist. Here, in Helen Keller, was a tangible, living reason to be optimistic in confronting the challenges that lay ahead.

Previously in Joe Miller, and now in Helen Keller, my father had encountered two figures for whom giving up was entirely incompatible with their DNA. To these two, giving up was as alien as hate was to Mother Theresa. With such inspiration, my father *had* to press on.

## 16

# MALCONTENT

FOLLOWING HIS SECOND TREATMENT AT Dibble and a brief stay at Letterman Army Hospital in San Francisco, my father's next stop in the Army medical system was Percy Jones Hospital in Battle Creek, Michigan. He was sent here to have his prosthetic legs refitted and improved, because the fitting at Bushnell had been less than perfect and had led to uncomfortable blisters.

His stay at Percy Jones was among the worst of his hospital experiences. This was surprising, as from the outside, the facility appeared far more impressive than the hastily built Bushnell and Dibble hospitals. It was a relatively ornate, 15-story building constructed by the Kellogg business dynasty,[159] and its patients included future U.S. Senators Philip Hart, Bob Dole, and Daniel Inouye.[160]

At Percy Jones, my father became something of a malcontent. This was due in part to his comparatively youthful age and the strict administrative regimen under which the facility was run. For example, the rules limited the wearing of civilian clothes away from the hospital or "off-post." Naturally, my father resisted and proceeded to break that rule more than once, much to the annoyance of his nurse. This seemed a little odd—why should a nurse care about what he wore off-post? The experience was perhaps exacerbated by the fact that Dad had had his fill of Army hospitals and what he considered their bullshit rules.

A nurse rescued my blind, legless father from the wreckage of a destroyed building; a nurse hooked him up to blood plasma when he was teetering on death; a nurse saved him from potential depression, and other nurses had done countless things to make his life more bearable. Yet, a nurse would not give him a toothbrush unless he paid for it, a nurse wanted to take his record player away, and now a nurse at Percy Jones didn't want him to wear civilian clothes off-post. Such were the stark contrasts that characterized my father's experience in Army hospitals. In a way, each set of contrasting experiences provided him with valuable lessons regarding how to treat and how not to treat people. These were lessons that Dad carried with him later on, when he could, and would, make a difference in many people's lives.

The clothes policy at Percy Jones was indicative of why, as far as my father recalls, morale was generally poor. Too many rules became a litany of indignities visited on banged-up veterans who were weary of being confined to hospital wards and subjected to insensitive and imbecilic policies. On one occasion, to temporarily alleviate the tedium and rigidity of the Percy Jones environment, Dad became his ward's liquor buyer. Granted an off-post pass, he hired a cab and went on a liquor-buying spree. Using some ingenuity, he asked the cab driver to stop by the hospital fence, and tossed the booze bottles over it onto the soft garden plants on the other side. With their newfound "medicine" the grateful veterans on the other end of this impromptu aerial relief effort got drunk. Thus, life at Percy Jones, with its indignities, was at least temporarily a little easier to bear.

Dad's uppity attitude, giving the "finger" to the "system" at Percy Jones, did not stop with the liquor. During the 1946 Fourth of July holiday, he discovered that his brothers Eddie and James were going to be in Dyersville, the latter having returned from a posting with the Central Intelligence Agency in the Pacific theater. My father asked for leave to go home. His doctor promptly denied the request. He gave no reason, just a curt "No, you can't go on leave." Dad's attitude and the doctor's genuine dislike for him probably had something to do with it. Unhappy with the doctor's response, Dad headed to the hospital's personnel office to appeal the doctor's decision. When he arrived, a personnel officer greeted him with the news that the doctor had already called and was adamant: no leave. The personnel officer said, "You're a combat-wounded veteran, aren't you?" Dad replied that he was. The personnel officer promptly granted him leave, along with a first-class train ticket back to Dyersville. Even within the bureaucracy that was Percy Jones, there could be the rational exception.

I could never picture my father as the Percy Jones malcontent he described. Perhaps it was the result of frustration accumulated during more than a year and a half in Army hospitals, dealing with bureaucracy and its bewildering manifestations, like the lieutenant who was worried about marked-up walls, the major who, by discharging him, was essentially going to toss him out on the street, or all the institution-first, soldier-second rules that he dealt with at Percy Jones. Whatever the case, m father had certain grown up and come a long way from small town Iowa and his Catholic upbringing.

## 17

# FACING REALITY

Dad's stay at Percy Jones was mercifully brief. Having made good progress with his walking, he was scheduled for more evaluation and rehabilitation for his limited vision. The reality was that his vision was still fading, and it would only be a matter of time before he was totally blind. Hence, he was sent to Valley Forge General Hospital, northwest of Philadelphia, in Phoenixville, Pennsylvania. Like the Dibble hospital in California, Valley Forge was an eye treatment center (among other specialties), and tens of thousands of veterans were treated here through the Vietnam War before the facility closed in the mid-1970s.

Valley Forge was a large, 2,000-plus bed facility with nearly 100 buildings spread over 182 acres.[161] It was situated in a picturesque part of Pennsylvania with rolling, forested hills, not far from the fabled encampment of George Washington's Continental Army during the Revolutionary War. At the entrance to the hospital was a parade ground with a two-story headquarters building, complete with a white cupola on top, at the opposite end. Both sides of the parade ground were flanked by similar two-story, red brick buildings, with several more arrayed behind the headquarters. The buildings had large paned windows and white trim, giving Valley Forge General Hospital the look of a college campus, which, in fact, it is today.

As was the case at Bushnell, the buildings were connected by enclosed corridors, allowing staff and patients to travel between buildings without ever having to go outside. The corridors and low ceilings give the place a rather claustrophobic, institutional feel, even with the large windows. Despite the pleasing facade,

Valley Forge was in reality a facility that had been constructed quickly to meet the exigencies of war. It was not a resort.

While at Valley Forge, my father resided in a 90-man ward for soldiers who had lost their sight. It was an environment that was familiar to him. While there, he began the process of learning the blind touch code, Braille, which is a system of raised bumps and symbols, each signifying a letter or number. By running their fingers across these dots and symbols, soldiers who had lost their sight learned to read.

These are the same kind of symbols that one might encounter today on an elevator button pad or hotel room placard. Individual letters are easy, but stringing them together is far more difficult. Some veterans mastered it, others did not. As my father described it, reading Braille was, like learning a foreign language, an activity better undertaken as a child rather than as an adult. However, Dad applied the same determination and perseverance to learning to read Braille as he had to learning to walk again. Nothing was going to stop him from doing the same things that "normal" people did. Given his love of books, he would not have it any other way.

Another key feature of the curriculum at Valley Forge was mobility training. This involved learning to swing a long, thin, white cane back and forth in front of you to detect objects in your path. Part of the syllabus involved navigating around the hospital and then the nearby town of Phoenixville. The latter could be hazardous because of the absence of architectural clues common today, such as the cut-outs on street corners that indicate to someone who is blind that he or she is approaching a street.

And there were other hazards, like partially opened doors on which a blind soldier could bash his face. My father's most vulnerable spot was just above the nose, where he still bears the scars of many encounters with doors. One of my earliest memories is of my mother directing us kids never to leave doors halfway open around the house.

"Obstacle perception" was another technique taught at Valley Forge, and this was depicted in the 1951 movie *Bright Victory*, which was filmed at the hospital.[162] *Bright Victory* is about a blinded soldier going through rehabilitation from wounds suffered during World War II. In a memorable scene, an instructor tells Sergeant Larry Nevins, the protagonist, that those without sight develop a sense of "obstacle perception" that allows them to sense nearby obstacles and prevents them from, say, running into a wall.[163] My father always chuckled about that scene, and assured us that he had no such "perception." Someone who suffered from vision loss would crash into walls, trees, and posts just like anyone else whose eyes were covered.

Tragically, this supposed "obstacle perception" was an example of many misconceptions that existed in the World War II and post-World War II eras, about those with vision loss. Such misconceptions often led to people with vision loss being consigned only to certain roles that narrowed their career choices and left many of their talents underutilized. My father was one of the fortunate exceptions. He simply refused to allow artificial limitations on what he could do, in spite of some of the prevailing views of the era.

As was perhaps the case with many wounded veterans in similar situations, my father's rehabilitation and entry into civilian life was not an upward arc of constant improvement. Instead, a series of obstacles and setbacks required course adjustments. In that sense, the wall which, in *Bright Victory*, was placed in front of the blinded veterans was a metaphor for the artificial obstacles that, however unintentional, would be erected in front of them by society.

Given my father's ready-to-move-on ethic, it would be easy to underappreciate the tragic effects of multiple wounds on some of his contemporaries. An insight into these effects was given in a *New York Times* account of the struggles of one young veteran at the Valley Forge hospital.[164] He was a young Army Air Force pilot whose transport plane had blown up while carrying a cargo of gasoline. The explosion badly disfigured his face and left him blind.[165] According to the newspaper account, all he wanted to do was die.[166] The only thing that saved him from self-destructive depression, and perhaps death, was a hospital volunteer who refused to leave his side.[167]

Despite hours of interviews on dozens of occasions, despair and lack of hope was not something my father wanted to talk about at any length. I suspect, though, that it was an omnipresent part of life in the hospitals. After all, these wounded veterans were generally young men in their early twenties who had undergone life-changing events under horrific circumstances. They had lost legs, arms, hands, feet, fingers, toes, genitals, and eyes, and suffered from nightmares. Lack of hope, despair about the future, and the associated aimlessness that it produced were not uncommon.

Helping to mitigate this, in my father's case, was the camaraderie with his fellow wounded veterans. Additionally, there was the fact that there were so many of them. This was combined with the overwhelming gratitude with which they were received in a society where the war was not some abstract event fought by someone else, or that was generally out of sight and out of mind. World War II impacted nearly everyone in some way. Whether it was a daughter or son who went into the service, the mother who worked outside of the home for the first time in a defense plant, the students who practiced air raid drills in schools, or the rationing for just about everything — sugar, rubber, meat, coffee — and the list went on.

The society my father adjusted to as a wounded veteran was far different to that of today's soldier returning home. Then, people seemed to understand the wounded veteran's mindset better than they do today (with some notable exceptions). In one instance, my father was boarding a crowded bus while in uniform. The driver abruptly announced that the bus wasn't going anywhere until someone gave him a seat. Someone did and the bus moved. On other occasions, while riding buses in civilian clothes and hardly able to see, passengers always offered him a seat. At first my father could not figure why, until he recalled he was wearing the Purple Heart pin on his lapel.

Such treatment did not stop there. Dad was sometimes

recognized, as a result of Frances Langford's "Purple Heart Diary" national newspaper column, and this followed him east to Valley Forge. For example, he received letters from a Philadelphia couple inviting him to their house in the city. On his arrival, the reason for the woman's interest in Dad became apparent. The couple had a daughter whom the mother was anxious to have him meet. Apparently, she was unhappy with her daughter's current boyfriend. Based on my father's appearance in the Purple Heart column, the mother thought he would be the perfect replacement. The awkwardness of the situation did nothing to deter her. Later, she offered to have her daughter drive my father back west to Missouri. He declined.

Overall, whether being offered a seat on a bus or invited to someone's home, it is hard to imagine my father receiving a similar level of treatment today. Many citizens may have no idea what a Purple Heart is, due to the more removed nature of the military from today's society and the drone-like, synthetic nature of the wars we fight—synthetic, that is, unless you are the one fighting them, or a loved one waiting at home.

---

I recently visited the site of Valley Forge General Hospital, which is now the University of Valley Forge. In some areas, it seems little changed from its days as a hospital, the red brick and white trim buildings echoing the facility's past. As I walked around, I thought about the patients who sat there contemplating their futures; soldiers with some sight and others with none at all. For some patients, it probably meant coping day-to-day while facing an uncertain future. For others, it was probably hour-to-hour. And for the lucky ones, such as my father, it probably meant being able to face each day with optimism about the future, even without knowing what there was to be optimistic about. I came away admiring them all.

The only explicit mention of Valley Forge's wartime past was a small, innocuous plaque in the ground provided by a local veterans' organization. It merely noted that the site was once a hospital.

I thought it ironic that many battlefields are full of monuments honoring heroic deeds, and rightfully so. Yet, places like Valley Forge General Hospital, where soldiers displayed heroism of a different sort, are memorialized only by a rudimentary plaque.

---

Although my father's stay at Valley Forge was brief, it marked a significant turning point. In an impulsive request, he asked to be discharged so that he could go to college and get on with life, even though he was not entirely prepared at that point to deal with his fading vision. Dad's request was perhaps brought on by a combination of his exhaustion with hospitalization, innate stubbornness, relative immaturity and perhaps some denial of the impact his loss of vision would have on him. The administrative officer asked him to reconsider. He declined. This was followed by requests to reconsider by his Braille instructor, his nurse, and then his ophthalmologist. The answer in every case: "No." Dad wanted out. He'd had enough of the institutionalization, enough of the instruction, enough of the rules, and enough of the goddamned Army.

As so often happened with my father, fate again intervened to move him ahead. In this case, the Army got it right in the form of an officer who presented him with military orders to report to Avon Old Farms rehabilitation center in Connecticut. Although weary of hospitals, orders were orders. So, it was off to Avon Old Farms, a place that would provide him with the skills he would need to go to college, and that ultimately would lead to another life-changing event.

## 18

# FINAL STOP AND DISCHARGE

Avon Old Farms was a rehabilitation center outside of Hartford, Connecticut, that served as a finishing school of sorts for blinded veterans. At this facility they learned the practical skills to get on with life outside of the military. Avon was an idyllic setting. The center had previously been a boys' school, consisting of stone and oak buildings in an Old English style.[168] The goal at Avon was to help veterans acclimate to society in a more relaxed, civilian-like environment. While there, my father became editor of the hospital newspaper (the *Avon Quadrangle*) and otherwise continued his Braille and mobility skills training.

At Avon, Dad also had — incredibly — his first and only visit with a psychiatrist. Considering his condition, it seemed odd that for almost two years after being wounded, he received no psychological counseling. In any case, it was perhaps just as well, because the resident shrink was immersed in writing a book and less interested in the welfare of the veterans, who tended not to take their interviews with him seriously, and sometimes used these sessions to have a little fun. For example, while he was interviewing my father, the psychiatrist brushed his own leg several times. So, my father brushed his as well. The conversation then went something like this:

> *Disinterested shrink (maybe hoping to extract something profound)*: So, why are you brushing your leg?
>
> *Wedewer*: Ah ... why are you brushing yours?
>
> *Disinterested shrink*: To get a bug off my leg.
>
> *Wedewer*: Well, I was brushing my leg to keep you

from brushing that bug onto my leg.

Later in the conversation:

*Disinterested shrink*: So, how is your sex life?

*Wedewer*: None of your business.

End of interview and end of psychological treatment.

A placement test designed to evaluate Dad's suitability for certain professions was similarly unsuccessful. It didn't help that the test administrator was smoking. As annoying puffs of smoke curled around his face, Dad had to complete one more damn evaluation. The test was easy to manipulate, and my father got even with the administrator by only taking it half seriously. The serious part was to answer the questions in a way that would show he was suited to be a journalist (he would try that later on). The not-so-serious part was to take an extreme, moralistic tone in responding to the questions, to subtly protest the "smoke treatment." The result: he was told he was also suited for the ministry.

While at Avon Old Farms, Dad dated a war widow named Moriarity. Her husband, an Army Lieutenant, had been killed in action not far from where my father was wounded, when the jeep her husband was riding in struck a land mine, and shrapnel from the blast severed an artery in his neck. The lieutenant's driver held his hand over the wound, trying to stop the blood spouting from it. But no matter how hard the driver tried, he couldn't stop the bleeding. Lieutenant Moriarity was gone.

Dad's dating relationships with her and other war widows never seemed built to last. The unsaid thing with my father was that he had been around enough sadness. However kind and caring the war widows he encountered were, I sense that he wasn't prepared to spend a lot of time around them or their sadness. Dad was young and had already experienced a lifetime's worth of sadness, and perhaps was unwilling to take on more. He and his dates were victims of the war, him physically and them psychologically. By some figures, World War II killed more than 400,000 Americans and wounded another 600,000. However, those numbers do not include the probably millions of spouses and family members who experienced lasting emotional and psychological trauma.

Dad did have positive memories of Avon Old Farms, though, mainly of the food and the parties. At one party, he met my mother, Marabeth Swanson. She came from Hartford with a group of other local young women to attend one of the many dances held at the center. Dad was supposed to pair off with someone else as was Marabeth. Instead, as fate would have it, they ended up sharing each other's company that night.

# 19

# MOM

MARABETH SWANSON GREW UP IN circumstances not unlike my father's. Her home was a modest, two-story house on Brunswick Avenue in suburban West Hartford, Connecticut. The most noticeable thing about the Swanson residence wasn't the house itself, it was the large elm tree that stood prominently in front, with the box-like house behind it, almost like an afterthought. The house was compact, with four bedrooms and a single bathroom. A second bathroom was later added in the basement. Behind the house was a work-shed from where her father, Harry Swanson, operated his plumbing, heating, and air conditioning business. In the driveway was Harry's work truck along with the family sedan, giving the Brunswick Avenue house the appearance of exactly what it was — a typical blue-collar, middle-class household in West Hartford.

Although West Hartford was a suburb of Hartford, Marabeth's upbringing there was similar to Dad's small-town roots. Although not overly so, both were influenced by ethnic and religious identity. The Hartford area was populated by a large Swedish-American contingent with strong ties to the Lutheran Church, in this case represented by Emanuel Lutheran Church. The church was a fixture in downtown Hartford, much like St. Francis Xavier in Dyersville. The Swansons on Harry's side, and Moranders on Marabeth's mother Ellen's side, both with roots in Sweden, had settled in the Hartford area several decades before. There they mostly remained.

Like my father, my mother had a generally happy and stable upbringing, considering the hard economic times during the Great Depression of the 1930s. Also like my father, she had in

Harry a strong, larger-than-life father who at times struggled with the difficulties of running a small business. When times were better, Harry, who started out as a plumber's apprentice, could afford to employ three or four workers. At other times, he could not. Fortunately, as was the case with my other grandfather, Ben Wedewer's general contracting business, Harry Swanson's plumbing, heating, and air-conditioning firm managed to survive during the Great Depression. As a result, the four Swanson kids always had food on the table and never lacked the basic necessities.

This was not an insignificant accomplishment during the epic economic calamity of the Great Depression. It was a time when nearly 25 percent of Americans were unemployed; when wage income for those still employed dropped more than 42 percent during a four-year period; when the banking system collapsed; when makeshift shanty towns sprang up for those who lost their homes; when farms failed across the Great Plains in the debilitating drought and storms of the "Dust Bowl;" and when towns were posting signs telling those seeking employment to go elsewhere.[169] That the Swansons and Wedewers managed to survive as intact families reliant on small businesses was particularly noteworthy, given that many Americans saw their livelihoods extinguished overnight in a torrent of crushing economic news that swamped the nation for over a decade. It was an unforgettable experience for all who endured it.

Marabeth's mother, Ellen, was more reserved than her father — perhaps a listener more than a talker. She was a cerebral, even-tempered person, and was not a confrontational parent, preferring to leave disciplining the kids to Harry. These qualities were by no means indicative of a meek person lacking inner confidence and determination. Instead, they helped Ellen overcome the circumstance of her upbringing, and equipped her to provide a stable, wholesome environment for her kids. Ellen passed those qualities along to Marabeth, enabling her to thrive and succeed.

Ellen's mother, Julia Morander, immigrated to America from Sweden in the late 19th century; no one is sure exactly when. She came to serve as a nursemaid to the wealthy Cheney family, who made a fortune in textiles in Connecticut. Ellen's father was a carpenter.

Although well read, and proficient in math, Ellen, or Nanna as she was affectionately known, never finished high school. Instead, at age 14, she quit school and went to work in a clothing store, to help with the family finances. Perhaps as a result of working here, and to distance herself from her relatively impoverished upbringing, Nanna always liked nice clothes, and dressed regally when she could afford to. She married Harry and subsequently settled in West Hartford, where they started a family.

Although part of the relatively insular Swedish-American community, neither Ellen nor Harry was defined by it. They were both born in America, and in settling in West Hartford, had a wide set of friends with whom they liked to socialize and felt at ease, whether they were considered "sophisticated" or not. Likewise, when business was good, Harry and Ellen took an occasional trip to New York City to attend the opera (during which, one time, Harry promptly fell asleep). Or, for a livelier, edgier evening, they might go to the Cotton Club, the famous jazz nightclub where the musicians and dancers were all African-American and the clientele was all white.[170] As a "speakeasy,"[171] the Cotton Club was a place where you could buy alcohol during Prohibition, when doing so was illegal, although most citizens largely ignored this ban.

These sorts of experiences perhaps characterized Ellen. She was someone for whom insularity and sameness among friends, places, and experiences was antithetical to her outlook. Denied any real education by circumstance, her intellectual outlets were books, art, music, and the card game bridge, which allowed her to employ her natural math skills. She ran her house and family well, but at the same time found working outside of it, when the opportunity arose, to be a liberating experience. Even though increasingly slowed by the lingering effects of rheumatic fever, an illness that would eventually lead to her premature death, Nanna pushed herself hard, particularly when it came to her children. Even during the Great Depression, Nanna's children were not going to lack home-cooked meals, decent clothes, swim lessons, music lessons, concerts, the occasional trips to the beach on Long Island Sound, and all the other accouterments of a normal upbringing.

In her personality, Marabeth reflected Ellen's experience and qualities. She too was well read, which compensated for not having any real opportunity to attend college. Like Ellen, she wasn't defined by a single experience or background, but rather was always open to new experiences and meeting new people. She was rarely judgmental about either. Indeed, Marabeth would come to thrive on both. The similarities did not stop there. Like her mother, Marabeth would come to push herself hard—very hard—when it came to her children. And although not controlling of her children, she became the consummate worrier about the things that mattered.

Ultimately, Marabeth, like Ellen, combined the worldly with the practical while being at ease with those around her. Both women were imbued with the ability to push themselves hard, along with possessing an inherent, live-and-let-live openmindedness. Through the qualities she shared with her mother Ellen, Marabeth would become a preeminent support system, and indeed an integral part of my father's future.

---

The Swanson home on Brunswick Avenue never lacked for visitors from the extended Swanson and Morander families, many of whom had colorful pasts. There was grandmother, Julia Morander, who managed to save enough money to invest in real estate in the Hartford area. This was not an insignificant achievement, given that she was paid the wages of a nursemaid. To safeguard her money, Julia deposited her money at seven different banks following a bank panic in the 1890s, when many banks failed. It was a time before bank deposits were federally insured, and perhaps for good reason, Julia did not trust the bankers.

Then there was Neil Swanson, my mother's grandfather. Neil was a farmer outside of Hartford—that is, until he was kicked out by his wife, who had already had enough of the farming life in Sweden. Instead, she wanted to open a boarding house in Hartford. Free of Neil, she proceeded to do so.

Finally there was Uncle Leonard, who fought in World War I and was rumored to have a steel plate in his head that made him a "little barmy."

As was the case with my father's family, the war changed everything for my mother's. Like the Wedewers, prior to Pearl Harbor, the Swansons were not keen to see the United States entangled in another overseas war. The Japanese attack changed all that. My mother's oldest brother, Arthur, although already attending The Citadel, The Military College of South Carolina, was drafted into the Army and first assigned to the coastal artillery. That assignment did not last long. He was soon reassigned to the infantry and sent to combat in Europe while serving in General Patton's Third Army. Her younger brother, Harold, barely old enough to serve, enlisted in the Navy and was sent to the engineering corps and on to the South Pacific theater of war. My mother's older sister, Harriet, became a nurse, while her mother, Ellen, went to work in a defense plant. Her father, Harry, became an air raid warden. In short, for the Swansons, like the Wedewers, it was all-in to support the war effort.

However, being all-in caused some strain in Ellen and Harry's marriage. With the war, Harry's plumbing and heating business fell on hard times, and the strain of the faltering business was exacerbated by having two sons overseas in combat. As a result, Harry moved out to work at a hospital, while Ellen worked at the Colt Firearms plant in Hartford. It was the first time Ellen had worked outside of the home in years, and she found the independence liberating. Marabeth was still in high school, and she stayed with her mother. Meanwhile, the family had to downsize their home, selling the house on Brunswick Avenue because of their reduced finances.

The Swanson family's experience was not unusual. That was what the war did to families. It changed relationships, tore them apart, rearranged them, opened new horizons, and led to heartbreaking tragedy. Its profound impact shaped family futures in large and small ways. Overall, though, even with the changes wrought by the war, the Swansons, like the Wedewers, were lucky in that no one was killed. But things were never the same.

---

After graduating from high school in 1946, Marabeth held several jobs, which were relatively easy to come by at that time. There was the job selling women's dresses at a department store; the clerk-typist job at United Aircraft, where her boss asked whether her job was interfering with her social life; working for the osteopath who, according to Marabeth was a "quack" who cheated on his spouse; working as a customer service representative for a phone company, where supervisors listening in on her calls thought she was too soft on customers; and working for an insurance company, the Hartford Accident and Indemnity Company. The latter job was generally how young Hartford women started out in the world, as the headquarters of several major insurance companies were based there: find a job at an insurance company, gather a wardrobe, meet a man, and get married. Under such circumstances, my mother's career choices were limited. She thought about going into fashion merchandizing, but decided it might be a bit too rough and tumble. She didn't seriously think about attending college, and in any case, this would have strained her family's finances.

Marabeth also dated a lot. She was outgoing, fun-loving and liked a good party. There were dates with West Point cadets, Annapolis midshipmen, a company pilot, fraternity brothers, and so on. Like jobs, dates were plentiful, and she had been dating since she was 14. At that age, a date meant your parents were in the front seat of the car and you and your date were in the back. This early start to dating gave Marabeth a certain insight into men. Her theory was that it was good to experience a "bum or two" in your dating life, to better sort the good from the bad. She did indeed experience at least one bum — the corporate pilot she dated before discovering he was married. He was instantly tossed.

Thus the bus trip to a dance at the Army rehabilitation center at Avon Old Farms, one night in the fall of 1946, was nothing new. It was just one of the many social events she attended.

Nor was the dance anything particularly new for my father. The Red Cross had fixed him up with a date, but soon after meeting her, someone he was more interested in, Marabeth, joined them. Dad sent out subtle signals to his fix-up date that two was company and three was a crowd. Dad was 21 and my mother was 18.

That night my mother told her family that my father was "the kind of man I'd like to marry some day." Given her active social life and impressionable young age, it was no surprise when they rolled their eyes. They felt sure this was another infatuation, sure to flame out. After all, she was only 18 with a lot of growing up to do.

What my mother may have lacked in maturity, though, she made up in perceptiveness. Like her mother, Marabeth had the gift of being able to quickly and intuitively size up situations and people, without being judgmental. She sensed in my father someone who was well grounded at 21, and who was optimistically looking to the future.

Thus, the anticipated flameout did not happen. As their relationship continued, her parents raised the inevitable question of how well-prepared she was to deal with my father's handicaps. My mother never hesitated. She was in love with Dad, and that was it. In retrospect, it was a bold decision. Until now she had been living a relatively carefree existence, and she was contemplating signing up to a partnership with someone who society was going to treat differently. No matter how sympathetic that treatment might be, it was going to be different, and at times would be the source of considerable frustrations and setbacks. To deal with that, my mother was going to have to mature quickly.

This was the source of whatever hesitation her parents may have had about her marrying my father. Was she really prepared to become the life partner of someone with handicaps? Looking at her life until now, carefree, and moving from job to job, Marabeth seemed an improbable candidate to take on such a responsibility.

The intervention of her levelheaded Aunt Elsa helped. Elsa's view, as imparted to my mother's parents, was that, had her own sons come back wounded, she would have wanted them to have every opportunity in their love life, whatever their wounds. Hence, whatever perceived immaturities my mother may have had, the fact that veterans such as my father should have a chance helped overcome her parents' misgivings. Before thinking about marrying, though, my mother and father decided it was best for Dad to get some college behind him. So for now, they decided to carry on a long-distance relationship.

---

In December 1946, my father was discharged from the Army at Westover Army Airfield in Massachusetts. Physically and mentally, he was a very different person to the one who entered the Army three-and-a-half years before. He matured a great deal in those years, most of which were spent in Army hospitals. During that time, he absorbed a lifetime's-worth of sorrow and tragedy. No one comes back from war entirely the same person. Yet, my father had adjusted to his circumstances. Life would go on, and he would begin anew.

Before the war he'd been interested in attending college, and was encouraged to do so by his parish priest. Now he was more determined than ever to attend. Perhaps it was the same animating force that motivated him to walk again: *the bastards that did this to me are not going to keep me down*. And perhaps it was his readiness to be free of the constricting institutionalization of Army hospitals. Whatever the cause, my father was ready to get on with life.

## 20

# OFF TO COLLEGE

COLLEGE WAS NEVER A PRIORITY for the Wedewers. My father was the only one of his brothers to attend, and as far as he remembers, none of his relatives went to college. This was something he attributed to their German heritage, which always seemed focused on accumulating more land rather than worrying about college courses. In their line of thinking, increasing your land and working it was how you made a living; education was not a priority. College was, however, something my father always aspired to.

Army service left him legless and mostly blind. It was through this service, though, that he now had the opportunity to attend college. In 1944, Congress enacted the first GI Bill, under which the government would pay for, among other things, the cost of college for returning veterans. Like the successor bill enacted for veterans of the wars in Iraq and Afghanistan, the original GI Bill provided veterans a chance to pursue an opportunity that was previously unavailable. This was particularly the case among the large number of World War II veterans who grew up in the economic hardship of the Great Depression.

For Dad, and many of the World War II veterans, the GI Bill, and the opportunity to attend college under it, was transformative. Further incentivizing him was the encouragement he received during his hospital stays. While at Dibble, for example, he was encouraged to attend Stanford University and was offered assistance in applying. Later, he was encouraged to apply to Princeton. But having felt bounced around the country for two years in Army hospitals, Dad was ready to return to the Midwest.

The University of Iowa seemed a good fit. It was, after all, his home-state university. When he visited, however, he was put off by the way disabled veterans were segregated into a separate dormitory, away from the general student population. My father didn't want to be a part of what he described as a "freak show." Decades before the mainstreaming of students with handicaps into the general student body became commonplace, he was ahead of the curve. He had an innate resistance to being pitied. Being felt sorry for, or made to feel like he was not a real student but instead was one of "them," was not something he was willing to let happen.

Then there was Marquette University, a well-known Catholic university in Milwaukee. There, a priest told Dad it was a settled matter that he attend — it was his obligation as a Catholic to do so. Dad's unstated response was, "Oh really?" Having been told what do in the Army for more than three years, and having had much of his life controlled by others, the priest's presumption, however well intentioned, did not sit well with Dad. No one was going to tell him which college to attend — not even a priest. There was no way was he going to Marquette.

Ultimately, he settled on the University of Missouri. "Mizzou," as it is known, was a natural fit. It was in the Midwest and had a highly regarded journalism school, as well as a respected history department. Both of these interested Dad.

Driving to Columbia along Interstate 70 from St. Louis to the east, I could immediately sense my father's attraction to the area. There are few curves in the roads. Everything is straight, which was a metaphor for my father's — and many Midwesterners' — outlook on things. No pretense, plain-speaking, and all on the level. In many ways, driving to Columbia was like driving to Dyersville. I suppose that, had Dyersville been a college town, it would have been Columbia. Conversely, had Columbia been a farming town, it would have been Dyersville.

Mizzou was a very welcoming place for veterans. The university's handbook for veterans aptly described Dad's and other veterans' situations: "He can ill afford to spend months or years finding his chosen field. Hence, all facilities must be placed at his disposal so that he may decide quickly and correctly what he is fitted for and may train for it as rapidly as possible."[172] Such was to be the case with my father. He was someone in a hurry and ready to start a career.

Starting college in 1947 as a disabled veteran, however, presented challenges. First and foremost was finding a place to live. With millions of veterans entering college under the GI Bill, colleges were overflowing, creating a massive accommodation shortage. For Dad, finding housing meant going door-to-door long before the era of "reasonable accommodations" for those with handicaps. There were not yet railings or ramps to allow a person with handicaps to get around.

Fortunately he met the Boggs, a gracious, welcoming couple who took in boarders. Like so many families, their lives had been altered forever by World War II—in the Boggs' case, tragically so. The war took their only son, John, who was a crewmember of a bomber that crashed at sea while flying a mission against Japan. As the Army Air Force subsequently told the Boggs, rescue planes overhead saw crewmembers from the downed bomber bobbing in the water amid life rafts dropped there for their rescue. Whether because of injuries suffered in the crash, exhaustion, or sharks, none of the crewmembers, including John, made it into the rafts. Then, they were gone. John's body was not recovered.

The more Dad talked, the more the Boggs liked him, and he was offered the hard-to-find room. He and the other veterans the Boggs took in may have had a therapeutic effect on the couple in helping them deal with the loss of their son. In any case, in the boarding house or anywhere around the Mizzou campus, you were never far from the tragic stories associated with the war. Seemingly, everyone had one. Whether it was a dead or maimed son, brother, father, uncle, or grandfather, or the mother, daughter, sister, or grandmother who left home to work or go overseas to serve in the combat zone, or the family uprooted to move out of poor or rural parts of America to find jobs in the defense industries, the stories and impact of the war would seep through generations of families and literally every aspect of life.

The other veterans at the Boggs' included Bob Metze, a transport pilot during the war who did some crop dusting on the side and who went on to fly with American Airlines. Bob was a likable guy who wore his flight jacket everywhere ... *everywhere*. To class, on dates—perhaps he even slept in it. Then there was Hank Sather, who flew 25 combat missions as a bomber tail gunner during the war. Hank majored in zoology and biology and later went on to become a college dean.

In the era before the removal of architectural barriers to people with handicaps, Dad had to overcome a number of physical (and psychological) obstacles at college. In retrospect it seems surprising that such barriers still existed, given the number of wounded veterans who were entering college. For my father with his prosthetics, this meant hoisting himself on and off the two buses to and from class, as well as navigating his way through ice and snow.

His days were generally the same: up around 6:00 a.m., eat breakfast, catch the first bus from the Boggs's house on Worley Street for a nickel, and then transfer at 9th Street and Broadway to the second bus. Usually he stood the entire way on the typically crowded buses during a commute that lasted about 45 minutes. There were more physical challenges on arrival at campus. He had to walk up 95 steps (he kept a precise count) to his study room in the Ellis Library. On prosthetics, the climb meant grabbing the handrail with one hand, swinging one leg to the next step and then bringing the second leg up behind it. (I climbed these same steps in 2010, and can attest to the fact that it was indeed a challenge.)

Then there was Dad's eyesight, which was now limited to "traveling vision," by which he meant the remaining vision in his one so-so eye was not strong enough for reading. Nonetheless, he was determined as ever not to let his handicaps get in his way. Obstinate as always, Dad decided he was going to drive, even with the hazy vision afforded by his one eye. New cars were scarce in the early years after the war, as industry gradually retooled to manufacture consumer goods instead of those in support of the war. Nonetheless, my father was able to buy a new Pontiac specially equipped with a vacuum clutch that allowed him to shift without having to push a floor pedal, significantly relieving the burden on his prosthetics. The clutch was awkward, with a delay between cause and effect, but it worked. Driving with his traveling vision was another matter. No one from the State of Missouri was checking vision too closely when it came to handing out driver's licenses, so although barely able to see, Dad somehow managed to obtain one. Subsequently, when he almost ran over a pedestrian on a crosswalk, his enthusiasm for driving disappeared. End of driving story.

More successful, albeit just as challenging, were Dad's attempts to overcome his lack of vision in the classroom. He was able to take notes, but they were barely readable. To overcome this, along with the lack of textbooks in Braille, my father used a series of readers—students paid 50 cents an hour to read his textbooks. The readers were able to record some of his notes on a disc-recording device that mimicked the larger LP record players of the day. Fortunately for Dad, because he scored well enough on screening tests in math, he was not required to take any math courses at Mizzou.

Dad's readers were also helpful in transcribing his class notes, because with his limited vision, his writing as he recalled it was generally a mess. Likewise his readers were a necessary part of taking exams. The reader would read the exam questions and take dictation from Dad for the answers. This process could add a layer of difficulty to the exams. He was fortunate, because among his readers was the student body president, Winston Martin, who would go on to be a Marine Corps fighter pilot during the Korean War and later a president in the university system in Maryland.

In retrospect, the fact that my father overcame all of the educational obstacles he faced is remarkable, given the absence of the modern accouterments of recorded books, electronic readers, and so forth. It helped that he fell in with a small clique of veterans who faced the same hurdles, including vision loss. This group became my father's social center after he and my mother were married, in February 1950. There was the former Marine, Gibb

Corey from Illinois, who lost both eyes when he was shot through the side of the head in the South Pacific, with, according to my father, not a scar to show for it. The military told Gibb he needed a wife and a dog, and Gibb hastily got married while recuperating in Philadelphia. When the hasty marriage didn't work out, he found another wife while in Columbia. There was Bill Winstead from a small town in Missouri, who contracted an eye disease while in Burma during the war and would go on to teach in the university system in California. Ken Guest, also from a Missouri small town, was in the group. Like Winstead, he had contracted an eye disease during the war. Then there was Bob Bottenberg, who was wounded in Europe. Bob worked like hell, and then worked some more. His biggest disappointment was getting a B in a course. The group also had a non-veteran, Gene Larantos from Boston.

Dad's major was in education with a focus on social studies and English. Subsequently, he obtained his master's degree in history with an emphasis in public administration. Each of these disciplines later provided a foundation for my father's career. For example, in describing the type of work one could expect in graduating with an education degree, the university handbook noted, "All positions require working continually with people. The ability to plan and instruct are required in positions. Research of some kind is usually a part of each job and the supervision is usually only general in nature."[173] This, combined with the fact that there was a shortage of teachers, particularly male teachers, made it a seemingly perfect fit for my father. Less encouraging, though, was the anticipated pay: $1,500 to $2,500 a year, which was low, even by late 1940s and early 1950s standards.[174]

---

While studying for his degree, Dad also continued to pursue his interest in writing. In the summer of 1947, he took a job as a reporter for two local newspapers in Waverly, Iowa: the *Waverly Democrat,* and the *Bremer County Independent Republican.* He lived at a local hotel, spending his days with a photographer who doubled as his driver, cruising the back country of Iowa looking for stories. He got the job through his old high school coach, Charlie Gephardt, who was now editor of one of the papers. Gephardt's journalistic standards were not unlike his adherence to athletic rules — rather loose.

There was, for example, the story about a dog at the local veterans' club, which cleared glasses and bottles from tables and put them in the correct place. After Gephardt's edit, Dad's story morphed into the "bartending dog," conjuring up images of a dog mixing and serving drinks and maybe even taking a tip or two. Then there was the story about a farmer who was bitten many times by rattlesnakes while reaping wheat. Each time, he apparently used hot chicken guts to suck out the poison, a cure that supposedly worked.

My father wrote serious stories too, including one about migrant workers, and another about a kid with dyslexia, which at that time was not ordinarily reported on. Generally, however, Dad described what he wrote as "bullshit."

Bullshit or not, the experience allowed him to continue writing and building his communication skills. But with his poor vision, typing on an old-fashioned typewriter was becoming increasingly difficult, and because of that, Dad ultimately decided that journalism was not for him.

---

During his time at college, while coping with his vision and mobility challenges, my father also focused on his strengths, one of which was public speaking. He entered a university speech competition and made it into the final three. This was the kind of experience that would serve him well in the future.

The topic of the competition was an issue my father had witnessed in the Army: racism. More specifically, competitors were to speak on whether to allow African-American students to enroll at the University of Missouri. As one of the final three contestants, Dad spoke to an audience of approximately 500 about why they should be allowed to do so. He did not win. Even decades later, he felt rankled about the competition, because he felt the winner's speech was based on a contrived, insincere appeal to emotion, compared to Dad's more analytical presentation. Dad was not given to showing undue amounts of emotion, but he could speak persuasively and with conviction as an advocate for an issue he believed in. Overall, I think the speech competition gave my father more self-confidence, and experience in organizing his arguments. It also gave him a sense of inner exhilaration that flowed from speaking publicly in support of a moral cause involving fundamental fairness and respect for human dignity. Ultimately, he would have ample opportunities to give many more such speeches.

Unlike the State of Missouri and the university administration, the student body at the University of Missouri was generally forward leaning in highlighting the fundamental injustice of the state's discriminatory "separate but equal" laws regarding African-Americans. Indeed, the words of my father's reader and student body president, Winston Martin, were prophetic in publicly endorsing a student government bill that disallowed recognition of student groups that discriminated on the basis of race or religion: "Which kind of society do we want? What kind of leadership do we want for that society? Do we want the society which is blighted by the curse of categorical discrimination? Or do we want one which can be proud of its achievements without hiding skeletons in the closet of human history?"[175]

The university atmosphere my father and other veteran students were part of at Mizzou did not engender a thoughtless, unquestioning adherence to the prevalent discriminatory laws of the day. Instead, students *did* question those laws, the impact of which Dad saw during his Army service. This questioning of such discriminatory practices was fairly forward-thinking, considering this was at least four years before, at the national level, the U.S. Supreme Court addressed school segregation. It also spotlighted that my father was fortunate to have someone like Winston Martin reading for him. Being around such a person, Dad could not help but succeed.

Less forward leaning, though, was the University of Missouri's policy regarding gays and lesbians. The university administration

## THE BRAVEST GUY

essentially treated them as suffering from a contagious psychiatric condition, and prevailing university policy was "to remove such persons, when identified, from the student body."[176] As was the case with racism, it was going to take a long time for the country to face that issue.

My father fit in easily, because his classes were generally packed with returning veterans. Photos from the period show classrooms (which appear similar in size to that of a mega-church congregation) full of veterans anxious to get ahead. Generally, they were serious students, seemingly ready for a fresh start.

In the 16-year period encompassing the Great Depression and the war, the country had experienced hardship and tragedy. Indeed, economic hardship and war were the only experiences many young veterans had known. Now, though, in the late 1940s and early 1950s, things were different. The United States was victorious and on the cusp of prosperity, which in turn bred optimism. That optimism, I think, was present at Mizzou, along with a sense of idealism, epitomized by Winston Martin's stand against racism. This combination created the ideal atmosphere for Dad to learn in. Instinctively he had always been, and still is, an optimist, and Mizzou with its strong academics was a perfect fit. He never had a strong mentor among his professors or academic advisors because he didn't need one. The best mentors were all around him, in the form of his fellow students ready to get on with life and looking forward to the future. My father would need that optimism in the years to come.

Like Dyersville, Columbia's and the University of Missouri's ties to the military ran deep. Perhaps the most noticeable landmark on campus was the gothic tower originally dedicated to the Mizzou alumni and students who lost their lives during World War I. It is a stone edifice approximately 140 feet tall, resembling something you might find in an English village. World War I was a searing experience for Mizzou and a country unaccustomed to large overseas conflicts. For the U.S.A., World War II was far worse.

Most stark for Mizzou was the loss of life during the latter war. Approximately 311 graduates and students were dead—

shot down, killed in training accidents, blown apart, drowned at sea, dead from some disease contracted in a far-off place with a name nobody could pronounce; and some, just gone. From an undergraduate study body of approximately 5,000 in 1941, the university lost more than 65 percent of its students by 1943, many of them to military service.[177] Grim numbers indeed. And probably not unique to Mizzou. By any measure, World War II was a brutal, wrenching experience. No institution was immune, and few people were not touched in some way. In this respect, the impact of World War II was starkly different to the impacts of later conflicts, as famously described decades later by then Secretary of Defense Robert M. Gates, who observed, "Even after 9/11, for a growing number of Americans, service in the military, no matter how laudable, has become something for other people to do."[178]

With this strong military association, and so many veterans on campus, it wasn't hard for returning veterans such as my father to connect with college life at Mizzou. Nevertheless, there could be awkward moments, and some traditions needed to change. For example, in observing his walk, one professor asked Dad if he suffered from a "football injury." *Ah, no.* Then there was the tradition of upper classmen whacking with wooden mallets unsuspecting students who had the audacity to walk across sacrosanct parts of the university green. With all the returning veterans on campus, that practice was ended in case someone who had been shot, sniped, rocketed, shelled, bombed, suicide bombed, booby trapped, torpedoed, or mined, might take the mallet and bash somebody with it.

Overall, the environment at Mizzou was one of contrasts that perhaps reflected those present in wider American society. It was a welcoming place for veterans ready to forget the horrors of war and move on. Yet, it was also a place that deprived African-Americans, including African-American veterans, and others its benefits. Ironically, the person who spoke at my father's graduation had, in dramatic fashion, already begun breaking down the racial barriers that created a moral stain on this nation—barriers that have yet to be overcome.

## 21

# ENGAGEMENT, MARRIAGE, AND GRADUATION

IN NOVEMBER 1949, AFTER BEING apart for long stretches over a two-year period, my father invited Marabeth to Washington, D.C. for a veterans' convention. In those days, a young woman did not meet a young man somewhere for a weekend. But my mother managed to secure her father's permission and off she went to Washington. There, she and my father became engaged at the historic Willard Hotel. Three months later, on February 18, 1950, they were married in St. Mark the Evangelist Catholic Church in West Hartford.

It was a simple 20-minute ceremony. Dad's family, fractured by the war, was represented by his brother Walter, who was best man. After the ceremony, lunch at a local restaurant, Les Shaw's Place, consisted of turkey, sandwiches, wedding cake, and "spiked punch." Then the newlyweds took a train trip west to Columbia and, because of a rail strike, spent their honeymoon night aboard the train. This was followed by a ride in the back of a bus in the middle of the night to Columbia, and then having to wake up a motel manager to get a room.

The next morning, my mother was up early, driving Dad to class. Then she moved his belongings into a newly built, small, single-bedroom apartment on Pershing Avenue in Columbia. The apartment was in a single-story duplex. It was basic, but they considered themselves lucky to have it. Even five years after the end of the war, housing for veteran students, particularly those who were married, remained scarce. Some were even still living in converted barracks and trailers.

For my mother, being in Columbia was an entirely new

experience in a different environment. She was now far removed from the close-knit family and Swedish community that existed in West Hartford. She may have been wondering what she had gotten herself into. Yet this was the sort of thing my mother thrived on: change, new experiences, and being around new people.

---

Four months after my father and his new bride married and moved to Pershing Avenue came Dad's college graduation day at Mizzou: June 9, 1950. The speaker was the President of the United States, Harry S. Truman. That day, Truman personified those qualities that Dad admired most and would later, in many ways, emulate. Humble, plain-spoken, and a man of character, Truman was a person of contrasts who always identified with ordinary people. In one instance he could enjoy a hearty, local lunch of Boone County, Missouri ham, green beans, potato salad, angel food cake, beaten biscuits and homemade rolls,[179] and in the next, play an impromptu piano excerpt from Mozart's Ninth Sonata.[180] Truman's combination of plain-spoken everyman demeanor and powerful intellect made him equally at home talking to a hard scrabble farmer or a Renaissance scholar.[181] Perhaps most appealing was that there was nothing manufactured about him. He was not boastful, nor was he a chameleon-like politician who repackaged himself in order to be more appealing to voters. Instead, Truman was completely authentic.

Truman's fearlessness as a politician led to one of the most courageous decisions of his presidency: his ordering of the desegregation of the armed forces. Frustrated that his civil rights program was stalled in Congress, Truman announced by executive order on July 26, 1948, "It is hereby declared to be the policy of the President that there shall be equality of treatment and opportunity for all persons in the armed services without regard to race, color, religion or national origin."[182] Although not fully implemented for several more years, Truman's executive order was historic. In an equally bold move a little more than two months earlier, and over the strenuous objections of nearly all of his advisors, Truman ordered the recognition of the newly founded state of Israel, 11 minutes after it was officially formed, thus making the United States the first country to do so.[183] Both were examples of Truman's unflinching manner of doing what he thought best for the country — despite what others might think and what ramifications it may have for his tenure in office. It was the sort of decision-making that would have parallels in my father's career decades later.

Returning to Columbia and the symbol of higher education in Missouri was perhaps a milestone of some significance for Truman. Having never attended college, and as the last president to date not to have done so, Truman was now received in the center of higher learning in the state. It was an environment far removed from his childhood and life over 100 miles to the west, in Independence, Missouri. There, Truman read 6,000 books before finishing high school at age 15.[184] Although his father was reputed to be the "best mule trader in Jefferson County," his series of financial reverses meant that college was never an option for Harry Truman.[185] Instead, he went to work running errands, washing windows at a local drug store, wrapping newspapers, working as a timekeeper for a railroad, clerking in a bank, and plowing on his father's farm where his mother bragged that he "could plow the straightest row of corn in the whole county."[186] Now Truman was receiving an honorary doctor of laws and admittance to the prestigious Phi Beta Kappa. It was worlds apart from his upbringing.

Likewise, for Dad, the graduation ceremony at Mizzou was a remarkable milestone for reasons not unlike Truman's, which he may not have fully comprehended at the time. For him, too, a college education was an unlikely proposition, coming as he did from a family that didn't value higher education and where no one went to college. Moreover, five-and-a-half years earlier, he was twice given up for dead. Since then, he'd endured two years in Army hospitals, had been offered exit ramps to easier career paths — and likely dead ends — by well-meaning people, and had adapted to going to college in an environment not always conducive to someone with handicaps. But here he was, getting ready to receive a college degree conferred by the President of the United States. It was heady stuff for a young man from Dyersville, Iowa.

Truman's visit to Columbia for the Mizzou graduation ceremony was naturally a big event. In contrast to the security-laden precautions that surround presidential visits today, Truman's detailed itinerary was published in the local newspaper. The Columbia police chief emphasized that "the [president's] motorcade would not be a hurry-up affair and that pedestrians along any part of the route would have ample opportunity to gaze upon the president and members of the party accompanying him."[187] The police chief further proclaimed, "We've set up a schedule that calls for progress at the rate of one mile an hour, both going to and coming from the stadium."[188] To be sure, Truman lived in what is now termed the presidential "bubble," but that bubble was quaint by today's standards.

On graduation day 1950, 1,752 graduates received graduate and undergraduate degrees.[189] It was the 108th and, until that time, the largest graduating class in Mizzou's history.[190] Strikingly, approximately 1,400 of those graduates were veterans.[191] The morning graduation was held in the football stadium and was covered live through a national radio broadcast. It rained, but this had little impact on the graduates' spirits.

President Truman did not disappoint. Although his speech is now at most a historical footnote, it was nonetheless substantive, and indeed groundbreaking. He spoke about big issues, including the role of the United States in the post-World War II world. The thing about Truman was that when he spoke, particularly on a topic as weighty as the United States' role in the world, he spoke with conviction. There was nothing superficial about him—he meant every word of it, a trait underscored by his Missouri twang that didn't rise and fall with inflections. With Truman, you just got it straight, and characteristically in monotone. Commenting on the speech, one newspaper observed: "These are not mere words, casual political phrase-making. Mr. Truman is deeply sincere in their utterance."[192]

In focusing on the role of the United States, Truman articulated a theme that would resonate today. He described a world in which the United States would have to exert as much economic leadership as it had previously done militarily. He told the graduates, "The world into which this college class is graduating needs that sort of constructive, creative leadership in foreign economic affairs"[193] and "I hope some members of this class will consider that endeavor."[194]

It was perhaps in his closing, though, that Truman was his most prophetic, in words that not only would ring historically true, but in many ways reflected the trajectory of my father's future:

> "Oh, I wish it could be my privilege to be graduated here today with you. How I wish I could see the next 50 years. We are facing the greatest age in history. Some of you will see a world of untold and unimagined wonders. Read Alfred Tennyson's "Locksley Hall." He saw the future about a hundred years ago. How much greater a future you face only the greatest imagination can foresee. Face it with courage, with ideals, and high moral conviction, and God will reward you."[195]

It was a fitting close to what was, even with the rain-abbreviated ceremony, a momentous occasion. For Truman, he had returned to Missouri in a position that was unimaginable years before. Similarly, my father was in a place equally unimaginable a scant few years earlier. It was a moment to savor, and for Dad, a point of inflection in his life. Although there would be untold obstacles to overcome, and his progress would not be linear, he was now much better positioned to face the future. It was a future that, as the President stated presciently, "only the greatest imagination can foresee."

---

After receiving his bachelor's degree in June 1950, my father went on to complete his master's degree at Mizzou, in history with an emphasis in public administration. By this time, the Korean War had started and young men and women were once again being called to serve in an overseas conflict. For some reason, this led Dad's landlady to matter-of-factly suggest to him that he "should consider going back into military service." After all, according to the landlady, he might still be of some use to the military. Minus two legs, with shrapnel still in his body, a disfigured finger, one glass eye and barely seeing out of the other, Dad had had his fill of military service. He politely begged to disagree.

## 22

# SOUTH FLORIDA AND NEXT STEPS

MY PARENTS' REASON FOR MOVING to South Florida was simple and commonplace—to escape the snow and cold they both knew growing up. After a brief stay in Durham, North Carolina, where my father considered pursuing a PhD at Duke University, they decided to head farther south. This decision was based in part on the advice of my father's professors, who suggested he would be better off obtaining some teaching experience before working towards a PhD. In considering how far south to go, my parents figured that if they were heading south, they might as well go all the way. So, South Florida it was.

It was of paramount importance to my parents to choose somewhere they could build a house and raise a family. By this time, their family was already started. My oldest brother, Todd, was about two, and the next, Neil, was on the way. After consulting Miami newspapers, my parents settled on Coral Gables, a suburban bedroom community that seemed an ideal place to raise kids. In Coral Gables, it felt like everybody was from somewhere else. It was also a time when young veterans like my father were starting families, building homes, and entering the work force while figuring what to do for the rest of their lives. The ease of fitting in and making friends made Coral Gables the ideal place to start out.

Before they could think about building a home, however, my parents had to find temporary housing. This in itself presented a challenge, at a time when kids could routinely be excluded from apartment complexes. After some searching, they settled in a two-bedroom apartment in the Coconut Grove area of Miami. Coconut Grove is now known as a trendy area of high rises, restaurants, and shopping. But in the early 1950s, it had none of these; instead it was a rather ordinary waterfront community. Home for the Wedewers was an apartment on Aviation Avenue in what was formerly military housing. The neighbors had colorful backgrounds. One was rumored to be the mistress of a Caribbean island nation dictator. Another was a Swiss mother with two children and several boyfriends on the side, while her Army husband was overseas. Then there was the landlord. He was the kind of person who, while my father was paying the monthly rent, demanded the extra nickel he said Dad owed him. Overall, Coconut Grove was not ideal, but it was temporary. And it was a start.

It was also time for my father to begin looking for a job. Gone were the heady days after graduating from Mizzou with a master's degree in hand and plenty of prospects. Now, in a circumstance all too familiar to today's college graduates with liberal arts degrees, my father was looking for employment in a job market that, while it esteemed veterans — particularly wounded ones — seemed strangely unready to accommodate them.

Such was my father's experience, at least initially. As a result, his professional career went sideways for more than a decade. He wanted to be a teacher, and with very limited vision and without tools to compensate, he substitute-taught in the Dade County public schools for three years. During this time, he filled in everywhere, substitute-teaching math on one end of the educational spectrum, and band and chorus on the other, even though he was not particularly talented at music. It was a job, though an erratic one. Typically, he received a call at around 6:00 a.m. to be at some local school by 7:30 or 8:00 a.m., and, after a hurried morning routine, was off.

The personnel officer promised Dad a permanent teaching job in the public school system, but for some unexplained reason this never materialized. While there is no way of being sure, perhaps she didn't follow through because she was uncomfortable having a teacher with handicaps in the classroom. How would he cope? What would the students think? What would parents say? Dad's talents and background as a veteran appeared to count for nothing. Allowing a person with handicaps to teach seemed to require thinking too far outside the box. Decades later, Dad's feelings about how he was treated were as raw as they were blunt: "She screwed me."

My father's prospects for permanent employment seemed to take a promising turn when he received a call from another disabled veteran and paraplegic who'd graduated from West Point. This veteran had insight into what he thought would be a perfect job for my father, as a transportation coordinator for the City of Miami. The position seemed a good fit for Dad. It was an opportunity for more predictable employment that would be far better for his growing family than the episodic and tenuous nature of substitute teaching. In any case, he was arbitrarily dead-ended in the teaching profession and the transportation coordinator job offered a chance for a fresh start. A job interview was scheduled and my father was eager for the new opportunity.

The morning of the interview, though, things fell apart. As my father was preparing to leave for the interview, he received a phone call from a physician who worked for the City of Miami. The doctor's curt message: "Don't bother showing up for the job interview." According to the doctor, my father, in his condition, was too expensive to insure under the city's health insurance plan. Dad offered to waive the health insurance. No, he was told, that was not possible. *You are too much of a risk. You could be too expensive to us.* No interview. No job. Twice wounded in combat and holder of two Purple Hearts, the combat infantryman badge and later the Bronze Star—none of that mattered. My father was just another rejected job applicant.

Dad's successive experiences in being effectively frozen out of a teaching position and then the civil service burned, and burned a lot. It was the kind of arbitrary and unfair rejection that was not easily forgotten. Perhaps inflaming the wound was the fact that, in the early 1950s, there were relatively few tools for holding employers to account for such discrimination.

The twin rejections easily could have resulted in my father engaging in a navel-gazing, self-immolating bitterness. But this was not his way. Instead, he filed the discriminatory experiences away as sources of motivation to be tapped in the future, to overcome nonsensical and arbitrary discrimination when he was better positioned to do so.

In a larger sense, a society that only a decade before was so supportive of veterans and the war—a "Good War"[196]—had, it seemed, yet to figure out how to accommodate those wounded in it. While offering a sincere "thank you for your service" to its wounded veterans, society's thank you was not necessarily translated into bold, imaginative thinking when it came to employment opportunities for wounded veterans. *That* kind of imaginative thinking would allow veterans to truly recover from their wounds by pursuing meaningful employment outside of those areas traditionally thought suitable for someone with handicaps. It took several more years, at least in my father's experience, before the country would rethink what employment opportunities should be made available to a person with handicaps. Dad would be a part of, and indeed would lead, some of that change. However, before doing so, he would have to take another professional detour and hit bottom again.

## 23

# SEARS AND HITTING BOTTOM

AFTER HIS FAILED ATTEMPTS TO secure a permanent teaching job and a civil service position, Dad's next job, in the mid-1950s, was working in customer service at the Sears department store chain. It was not a great job, but it was work. Importantly, Sears, which sold a wide array of consumer goods ranging from washing machines to children's clothes, provided an atmosphere in which my father was able to develop his people skills. He started in sales, but quickly discovered sales was not for him. So, it was over to customer service where he answered phone calls from generally irate Sears' customers.

The late 1950s and early 1960s were similar to present-day, in that new consumer gadgets were flooding the market. In perhaps a precursor to today's consumer-driven economy, Americans in this era were well adept at accumulating stuff. Retailers like Sears fed this insatiable appetite for new devices and, rather like Apple today, seemed to anticipate what customers wanted even before they knew it.

Most prominent among the new gadgets was the television. The picture in those days was to varying degrees full of horizontal lines. At times, this produced weird contorted screens where the lower half of someone's face appeared on the upper half of the screen, while the upper half of their head appeared on the lower half of the screen. It was like watching a scene out of a horror movie. The reason behind those lines was open to interpretation.

For one older woman—a frequent caller to Dad's desk—it was all very simple. The reason for the distorted television picture was the Russian satellite *Sputnik*[197] orbiting overhead. Her theory was that the Russians were using the satellite as an insidious device for jamming American televisions. It was a plot, no doubt, to keep those well-heeled and undeserving American consumers from enjoying game shows and cigarette commercials, and, later, shows with talking horses or flying nuns, or my parents' favorite commercial, a scrawny guy dressed in several layers of business jackets that he would fling off one by one, as the announcer said how good each jacket would look on the viewer.

For another of my father's frequent callers—in this case a retired Army Colonel—the television picture was never "quite right." Never quite right, that is, when you've had a few drinks. Dad couldn't help with that one.

Other new Sears products pushed on consumers incorporated technology that, to put it euphemistically, still needed to have the bugs worked out. One was the self-defrosting refrigerator. It seemed as if the self-defrost was always one step behind the frost, creating an igloo-like effect. Out of frustration, unhappy customers used ice picks to break-up the frost. Unfortunately, the ice pick often penetrated the cooling coils, meaning the refrigerator was essentially toast.

Then there were the natural gas ovens with pilot lights that frequently broke. When the unlucky owner struck a match to relight the pilot light, they were often treated to a blast—and singed hair.

Then there was the combination washer/dryer that did neither very well.

My father's descriptions of Sears' misfires were the sort of thing that personal injury and product liability lawyers today dream about, and it is perhaps a wonder that Sears was not bankrupted by some of the technology they were selling.

Part of my father's job involved dispatching Sears service technicians to customers' homes, sometimes with amusing results. There was the time a customer heard rattling in her washing machine or dryer, which turned out to be an empty gin bottle she was trying to hide from her husband. Then there were the service calls in which the caller asked for a certain technician to come over. After a while, Dad figured out that a little afternoon sex was perhaps being provided along with the appliance repair.

My father was also responsible for selling service policies on the appliances. For televisions this was easy, because they broke on average once a month. Of course, the important thing was to sell policies on the stuff that *didn't* break.

Overall, though, Dad's Sears job wasn't bad. The work and his hours were steady, giving him time to spend with his growing family that would eventually number five children: my brothers Todd, Neil, and Donald Jr., and my sister Mary Ellen, with me as the youngest. Furthermore, my father's job at Sears, combined with his veteran's benefits and disability income, allowed us to go to Catholic schools and build a house on Catalonia Drive in Coral Gables, and then, later, to buy a four-bedroom, three-bath house on Country Club Prado.

My parents' intuition about Coral Gables being a great place to raise a family proved correct. It was a safe environment with lots of kids, broad sidewalks, places to play, accessibility to good schools, and people who, having come from everywhere else, were anxious to know their neighbors. While we were by no means rich, my father earned enough for us to take summer trips, including a long camping trip all over the East Coast and up to Canada.

Working at Sears for eight years also allowed Dad to develop his people skills. After all, there was no better way than having to deal with an irate consumer who had just discovered their newfangled gadget was not all that was promised. Walking such people back from their anger and frustration was a skill that would help him later in life.

Before Dad had an opportunity to further employ his people skills, however, he took a step backwards. In March 1964, the retina in his remaining eye detached again. Doctors tried to reattach it, but after so many previous operations, it would no longer adhere to the back of his eye. He was now totally and permanently blind. He came home, sat for three days pretty much by himself, and processed the fact that he was not going to see again. No traveling vision. No gauzy images of his kids. Nothing. Gone.

My mother left him alone during this period, knowing that as someone who did a lot of living in his head, my father was going to have to work it out on his own. At the end of three days, her message to him was stark: "You can either slit your throat or move on." It was the sort of stark challenge that perhaps only a dedicated spouse could throw down.

It was a challenge my father needed to hear. By his own inclination, and as a veteran, he was not susceptible to debilitating self-pity. My mother's presentment of his options, however stark, I think crystallized what he knew to be true. He was going to have to move on, if for no other reason than he had five kids and a spouse relying on him. *He had to move on.*

But not before things became even worse. About this time, Dad started to suffer from severe stomach pains. After several doctor visits, he learned his gallbladder had to come out. He'd been planning to take courses at the University of Miami to enhance his résumé, but those plans were now put on hold — as it turned out, for good.

No eyesight, screwed-up stomach, no near-term prospect for further education, a career that at best was going sideways, if not headed downward, and five kids and a spouse to support. My father's life was cratering. It was a moment akin to when he first lost his sight. Now he hit the wall again. Call it a funk, a depression of sorts, or something else; he was not progressing as planned in life.

At this point, as always, my mother was the hero. As had been the case at other turning points in my father's life, he was fortunate to have someone step in to keep him moving forward. This role came naturally to my mother. Like my father, she has always had an innate sense of optimism that serves as a propellant of sorts. A propellant that acts like an internal cup of coffee, allowing someone to quickly bounce back after a night's sleep or a long walk or a few chapters of good book. Also, like my father, she has an almost visceral counter-reaction to negativity. This is not to be confused with a contrived sense of "everything is just great, isn't it?" Instead, my mother had a natural ability to accept things as they were, recognize what was important, and then move on. Indeed, it is these qualities that have always made my mother so well liked. She just cannot offend.

Now that my father was totally blind with no prospect of his sight coming back; was recovering from surgery, and was not going back to school, he had to answer the fundamental question posed by my mother: "What now?"

## 24

# THE CALL TO PUBLIC SERVICE

IN 1968, "WHAT NOW?" FOR Dad was employment as a counselor trainee at the new Veterans Administration or VA hospital in downtown Miami. By this time the country had become deeply involved in the Vietnam War, and as a result the VA system was starting to care for veterans wounded in that conflict. Dad's job as a caseworker was to counsel wounded veterans adjusting to civilian life. In the absence of formal training, he did have two qualifications that ideally suited him for such work: he identified with his clients and he was invested in their success.

One of my father's first clients was Bob Andrews, a young Marine who was blinded in combat in Vietnam. The thing about Bob was that he hadn't needed to be in Vietnam. He had a college engineering degree and a promising future. Yet, in an era when young men were still drafted for military service, Bob volunteered for the Marines after finishing college. While scouting ahead on an operation, he triggered a booby trap. There was a flash and his sight was completely gone. It was the sort of circumstance that easily could have led to bitterness—questions such as, "What was I doing there in the first place?" or, "Why me?"

In Bob's case it did not. Dad described him as an even-keeled person who accepted his situation. He started with the basics, such as learning Braille, and eventually went on to a successful career as a general contractor, had a family, and even took up golf. Indeed, golf is an endeavor open to those with vision loss, and this is promoted through a flagship organization, the United States Blind Golf Association, whose website proclaims "You don't have to see it ... to tee it!"[198] Bob Andrews certainly didn't. He went on to win the national championship for blind golfers, and in 2009 was inducted into the Association's Hall of Fame.[199]

In some ways, I think my father saw a bit of himself in Bob Andrews, as someone who was level-headed and who kept a positive attitude even though dealt a hard set of circumstances. He described Bob as a "beautiful person." My father could offer no higher compliment.

Through his experiences with clients like Bob Andrews, the VA proved to be a great place for my father to begin his career in rehabilitation counseling, and one that would pave the way for his future success. Regrettably, though, the environment at the VA at times exhibited the same stifling bureaucracy he had experienced in Army hospitals, that only served to destroy patient morale. One such practice was the pill line up at 9:00 a.m., one day a week. This was the only time when veterans could get prescription refills. Not surprisingly, the lines were huge, akin to those you might see in food and water lines after a natural disaster. There was no real reason for the once-a-week policy, other than staff convenience. Imagine you had frozen your butt off in Korea while Chinese and North Koreans were trying to kill you, or had been eaten alive by bugs in Vietnam while North Vietnamese or Viet Cong were trying to kill you, or had served on some decrepit Navy ship where the elements, or the cooks, or the person making the "fresh" water was trying to kill you — you were still going to have to line up at 9:00 a.m. to get your pills at the VA. My father's verdict on the 9:00 a.m. pill line-up: it was a good deal for the VA employees, but it was a crappy deal for the vets.

Dad's job at the VA was meant to be only temporary, and he was fortunate in that around the same time, the Florida Council for the Blind (later called the Bureau of Blind Services and then the Division of Blind Services) was looking for an entry-level counselor. The council was the state agency created to serve the unique needs of the blind and visually impaired in Florida through services including vocational training and employment, assistance in formal education, transportation, development of life skills, and access to library materials.

The council owed its existence, in part, to Helen Keller, who did so much to advance the cause of those who were blind, or blind and deaf. In 1925, as an international figure, Keller was invited to Florida by supporters of the bill in the Florida Legislature to create what later became the Division of Blind Services. Through her trademark persistence, 16 years later, in 1941, Keller was again in Florida, urging the passage of a bill that would create an independent agency to serve those who were blind. Through her inspirational speech to the legislature, Keller helped push passage of the bill over the finish line. She provided the same sort of inspiration to my father five years later, when he was a young, wounded veteran wondering what his future would hold. Now, through my father's service at an agency that Keller helped create, their paths crossed again.

Helen Keller once said, "The chief handicap of the blind is not blindness, but the attitude of seeing people towards them."[200] That was the case in Florida. After initial progress in the state, the aspirations of its comparatively large population of blind and visually impaired individuals were stagnating, limited by low expectations and stale thinking about their capabilities. Historically, persons with vision loss in Florida were largely consigned to small-scale manufacturing jobs—making mop heads, bank bags, and the like. It could be a rewarding career, just like any other manufacturing job in America—if that is what one chose to do. The problem was that with few exceptions, it was the *only* form of employment generally available to persons with vision loss. However unintended, their treatment by those who served them had, in essence, developed into a subtle form of discrimination that essentially said: "We know what's best for you." The system worked in that it provided employment, but at the same time it channeled them into one line of work, effectively foreclosing all others. Compounding the problem of limited opportunities and independence for those with vision loss in Florida was that the Florida Council for the Blind itself became snarled in fractious infighting,[201] and as a result, "did not enjoy a favored status within state politics."[202] The council was dissolved as an independent body in 1969.[203]

By the time of Dad's employment at the council in the late 1960s, the agency and the treatment of those who were blind in Florida were ripe for change and new thinking. What was needed was a change agent whose background could engender respect among disparate groups.

That person was Don Wedewer. As a relatively young, disabled veteran, he had not only the experiences that could inform new ideas, but also the determination and persistence to bring them to fruition. My father also had the necessary organizational and management skills, and he understood people and what motivated them. Most importantly, he cared deeply about his clients and was ready to serve them with the same unwavering persistence that served him in his long recovery from his wounds.

All of these qualities and experiences were brought to bear on my father's signature project of the time — one that catapulted his career. It was a program to train people with vision loss to become service and claims representatives for the Social Security Administration, handling complaints from the public regarding their Social Security benefits and related service issues. Today, it doesn't seem particularly surprising that someone with vision loss would be considered for such work. But in the late 1960s, the concept was groundbreaking. If the training program was going to happen, and people with vision loss were going to have a new career path opened to them, it was going to require someone with a single-minded willingness to overcome long-held perceptions and prejudices about what those with vision loss were capable of. And, it required someone with a willingness to risk failure.

The role fit Dad perfectly. He developed the idea for the Social Security training program while still working at the VA. With the support of a VA psychologist and mentor, Dr. Mabel Gibby, he showed up on the doorstep of the Social Security office in Miami in June 1968. The supervisor there agreed to allow him to try working as a service representative to determine whether a person with vision loss could do the job.

It was a pivotal moment. If Dad failed, this would confirm the long-held prejudice that people with vision loss were capable only of certain manufacturing jobs and were unsuited to do anything else.

No special provisions were made for my father, other than a recording of the service representative manual, so he could learn how to answer questions over the phone. Other than that, he learned the job the old-fashioned way: through on-the-job training. After two months, he demonstrated to the local Social Security Administration management that a person with vision loss could do the job. Management was so impressed that they offered my father a full-time position as a service representative and were receptive to the idea of training more people with vision loss for the position. Dad declined the offer because he had already accepted the counselor position at the Florida Council for the Blind, but, in his parting words to management, he stated that he would be back in a few weeks. It was a bold statement, considering he was starting a new, entry-level position at the Florida Council for the Blind and did not even have the council's approval for such a program.

Strangely, when Dad took his proposal for a training program to his new employer, they were cool to the idea. Another training program for those who were blind? As service representatives? Over the phone? It seemed a bit out-of-the-box and did not conform to what people with vision loss traditionally did, i.e. assemble things.

The traditionalists were skeptical that people with vision loss could succeed in employment outside of manufacturing. At one point, my father was told by all three of his supervisors, including his agency head, that there were simply not enough qualified people who were blind to fill the nine or ten slots in a prospective training class, therefore such a program couldn't work. With characteristic persistence, Dad responded by providing his supervisors with a list of candidates for the training program, consisting of persons with vision loss who had earned college degrees. Curiously, it was more than six decades since Helen Keller earned her college degree with high honors as a blind *and* deaf person. Yet, to some in the Florida Council for the Blind, it was apparently a revelation that someone who could not see could still earn a college degree.

In retrospect, the traditionalists' resistance to my father's idea for a Social Security Administration training program seems incomprehensible. After all, if you were a Social Security recipient, you didn't care whether the person helping you on the other end of the phone could or couldn't see, or for that matter whether they had eyes in the back of their head, or horns coming out of their ears. All callers wanted was their problem solved—*and their damn money*. And this wouldn't be the last time Dad encountered such narrow thinking regarding how the visually impaired were supposed to be employed.

The sort of resistance he encountered could be called a bureaucratic "soft kill." Essentially, it was an attempt to kill the training program even before it started, by passively denying it any money, with the excuse that there were other priorities. Without money to support the program, and up against passive, and not so passive, resistance within the Florida Council for the Blind, my father nevertheless pressed ahead.

By December 1968, as a nearly brand new employee of the council, my father had organized an interagency meeting to work out an agreement for the program to proceed. To overcome the lack of funding for developing training materials, he enlisted the help of my oldest brother, Todd, in high school at the time, who spent hours recording some of the training on audiotapes. Todd's price was right: free. The outcome was not a high-end or elaborate production. Instead, it was a teenager reading training materials aloud into an old-fashioned tape recorder. Although it may have seemed odd for the Social Security trainees to hear a youngish-sounding voice reading the arcane training manuals, it worked. Additionally, Dad obtained support from mothers in the local Jewish community. Historically, they had a strong interest in supporting persons with vision loss, and helped translate the voluminous Social Security training manuals into Braille so that blind trainees could read them.

Dad worked with Dr. Gibby to develop a psychological test to ensure the initial trainees were of the right temperament to handle irate customers. More than anything, he wanted to make sure this first class of trainees would have a high graduation rate to fend off the skeptics who likely would have shuttered the training program had it not. Dad's persistence once again paid off. The high success rate among the initial class of graduates quieted the skeptics. During his tenure, the Social Security Administration graduated more than 150 students in 13 training classes in the Miami area alone.[204] The Social Security Administration was so enthusiastic about the training program my father started that they replicated it in regions throughout the eastern half of the country. Dad was subsequently called to some of those other regions to discuss the program, as well as to the national headquarters of the Social Security Administration in Baltimore to meet the agency head. Additionally, the training program was replicated in a least one other federal agency.

Begun on a shoestring, without funding and management support, the Social Security Administration training program started by my father, and the programs that sprang from it, were a terrific win-win: people with vision loss were given a chance for a career path that was previously off-limits to them, while the federal government ultimately gained hundreds of dedicated and highly qualified and motivated employees.

On another level, I think the Social Security training experience ingrained in my father the essential ingredient of successful public service: measuring your success through the success of others. To this day, he still recalls it as being his most rewarding experience while working on behalf of people with vision loss. It also, I think, taught him that even as a relative neophyte in government service, his ideas, combined with a strong sense of purpose, could make a real difference in the lives of others. Finally, it taught my father that if he wanted to achieve anything for people with vision loss in Florida, he was going to have to be bold.

Around this time, Dad achieved national recognition when he was featured in a publication developed by the President's

Committee on Employment of the Handicapped, entitled "Performance." The report described how quickly my father made a name for himself:

> "In a very short length of time, this multiple handicapped man has achieved a high degree of professional competence that demands the respect of his colleagues as well as providing the inspiration for the disabled people whom he counsels. For Don, his life is rapidly attaining the potential that hides in many men who do not have the perseverance to realize it."[205]

The Governor of Florida, Claude Kirk, was equally effusive in his praise of Dad: "I am overwhelmed by your personal courage and initiative ... Your life is an inspiration to many others ... Although the path has not been easy for you, through sheer perseverance you have accomplished what many with no handicap have been unable to do."[206]

In addition to these recognitions, my father received a presidential citation from President Richard Nixon and was named the Outstanding Handicapped Worker of the Year in Florida for 1970, as well as the Outstanding Blinded Veteran for the same year. A newspaper photograph of Dad seemed to capture it all: seated behind his Braille typewriter at work, he is wearing a big smile that exudes satisfaction with his work and hope for the future. Twenty-five years after the war, after years of working in jobs with no real future, and five years after again hitting bottom, Dad was plainly in his element. As he told a newspaper at the time, "Oh, I'm not happy about being handicapped, but I'm not bitter ... There are things to do."[207]

---

Aside from my father's more high-profile work with the Social Security training program, his official title at the Bureau of Blind Services, as his agency was now called, was Vocational

Rehabilitation Counselor, or working in "voc rehab" in the vernacular of the profession. The hours could be long, the clients sometimes difficult, and the neighborhoods he visited to serve his clients, rough. But Dad had an innate sense of caring, or more plainly, he gave a damn. As Helen Keller once said, "It is the caring that matters. The gift without the giver is bare."[208] Keller's words recognized that without this essential quality, one simply could not succeed in serving people with vision loss. Just as importantly, my father was willing to break through outmoded paradigms that hindered services to those with vision loss, something not always done in the vocational rehabilitation field. But to be successful in voc rehab, he had to.

The first step in providing assistance was to register the blind with the agency, and then to assess their needs and skills. As in the case of sighted people, a lower education level generally made placement in job training and ultimately a job more difficult. It was all about finding the right fit for the individual. One of the greatest challenges my father faced was convincing employers that people with vision loss could work in jobs where traditionally they were not considered employable. That took some doing.

Dad's work ethic, client commitment, and willingness to run with new ideas earned him quick promotion. In 1970, he was promoted to Placement Specialist, meaning he was in charge of finding jobs throughout the state for people with vision loss. Although the placement job was normally performed out of the capitol in Tallahassee, Dad convinced his managers to allow him to continue to work in Miami, where most of the growth in the state was occurring at that time.

The job was a perfect for my father, because it allowed him to apply his singular focus on opening new career paths for people with vision loss to a larger set of occupations and potential employers. It also allowed him to capitalize on his aggressiveness in serving his clients, as well as his ability to innovate. In the early 1970s, before the passage of national laws prohibiting discrimination against the handicapped, such skills were important, because the attitude of many employers in hiring people with vision loss ranged from skepticism to outright resistance. To help overcome this, Dad often offered employers trial periods with employees with vision loss. During these periods, the Bureau of Blind Services paid the employees "maintenance money" for their room and board, while the employers received the benefit of essentially free labor. At the end of the trial period, employers could still refuse to hire the employees. Some did, others did not. It was an instance where Dad overcame barriers, one employer at a time, one employee at a time, to advance the cause of those suffering from vision loss.

As he had as a counselor, my father excelled at job placement. In 1972, he was made a District Director, in charge of services to the blind and visually impaired who resided from West Palm Beach south to Key West. This was soon followed by promotion to District Supervisor, which meant that he had other supervisors working for him. Many of the counselors and social workers employed by my father during this time were young and idealistic. It was a heady time to be in such work, and to be taking on the "establishment" or "system," as the nation started to come to terms with the fact that it disenfranchised so many groups from full opportunity, including those with vision loss. To these young employees, prejudices of an unfair and uncaring society that led to low expectations, dependency, and limited hope had to be eradicated. Some of these employees could perhaps even be called zealots in their advocacy for those with vision loss. They were willing, and perhaps even eager to confront employers who were unwilling to offer opportunities to the blind and visually impaired. Dad served as a tempering influence on such employees. While he had certainly proven he was ready to take on the system in support of those with vision loss, he was unwilling to do so in a way that would alienate the very people whose minds he was trying to change.

Among my father's employees during these years were veterans from the still ongoing Vietnam War. Some worked out and others did not. Among the former was an Army medic who Dad hired as a counselor even before he left Vietnam. Another, who did not work out, was a former Marine who was never able to overcome his baggage from the war. As a counselor, he became overly invested, and perhaps emotionally consumed, in the needs of his clients. His zealousness progressed to a point where it interfered with his sound judgment regarding his clients' overall needs. To what extent this was due to the weight of the war, nobody could know.

After the former Marine was dismissed, word circulated that while in Vietnam he had "fragged" a superior officer. Fragging is military parlance for killing an officer whose incompetence you thought was going to get you and your buddies killed. Although perhaps not widely talked about, fragging happened in Vietnam — and in other wars. In this case, the young Marine, according to the story, drew the short straw among his fellow Marines and tossed a grenade into the officer's tent. That was that. Whatever occurred, while in my father's employ, the young veteran spiraled into drugs and emotional issues from which he never recovered. For Dad, this represented a failure in terms of assisting someone who, like him, was irretrievably altered by the trauma of war.

---

After his successive promotions in the early 1970s, my father continued to be bold and was willing to take risks to secure better treatment for those suffering from vision loss. When presented with an emergency in which surgery was required to repair a young man's detached retina and save his sight, my father authorized the commitment of funds even though there was no formal contract with the hospital where the surgery would be performed. His agency head subsequently told my father that he could be fired for committing the funds to save the man's sight. Dad responded with his characteristic directness: "Was it the right thing to do?" His agency head agreed, it was the right thing to do.

He made an equally career-risking move when he cut off funding for a training program run by a national non-profit organization that was treating visually impaired trainees as "a bunch of invalids," as my father put it. Dad was subsequently threatened by the local non-profit president, who said he "had friends in Tallahassee," the state capitol of Florida. It was not an idle threat. The local non-profit president did indeed have "friends" in senior leadership in state government, along with the power of a national organization behind him that could make life very tough for my father.

Dad's characteristic response was equally blunt: "Fine, call your friends." The non-profit president promptly did so, and soon Dad's direct supervisor, the head of his agency *and* the division head — his boss's boss's boss — were flying to Miami to resolve the non-profit funding issue. In an apparent end-run around him by his supervisors, Dad was not invited to the meeting. Perhaps they were uncomfortable with his boldness and matter-of-fact views. It took the last-minute intervention of the highest-ranking person attending the meeting, the division director, to get my father invited. It was another one of those pivotal moments in Dad's career where, by taking a principled stand, he was putting his career on the line. In this case, if the meeting did not go well, his future at the agency was at significant risk.

My father won the day. Even without the support of his direct boss and the agency head, both of whom backed the non-profit, Dad's unemotional laying out of the facts persuaded the division director that the blanket contract with the non-profit was over. Going forward, the non-profit was provided with a per-service fee, to ensure the organization was more accountable. The bottom line was: you want to get paid, don't treat people with vision loss as essentially good-for-nothings. It was perhaps an innocuous, but still important victory, sending a message that in Florida, the old ways of segregating those with vision loss into one field of work and then treating them poorly were over — all in large part because a guy left for dead on a battlefield over 25 years before was persistent enough and bold enough, in a quiet way, to make a difference.

To its credit, the Bureau of Blind Services, as it was now called, recognized that Dad's boldness indeed achieved results. In 1974, he was named the director of the bureau and moved our family to Tallahassee to assume the directorship. It was an impressive accomplishment: he had been elevated from an entry-level position to head of the agency in five-and-a-half-years. Now, he was in charge of approximately 330 civil servants, in addition to more than 500 enterprise employees who managed snack bars in public buildings as part of a public-private partnership, and a $44 million budget. Most importantly, my father was charged with providing services to tens of thousands of people with vision loss in Florida, which had one of the largest populations of blind and visually impaired citizens of any state in the country.

Dad's guiding philosophy was not that of a radicalized handicapped person ready to smash a lot of china (although the resistance of some to people with handicaps may have at times justified it). Instead, he brought a persistent determination that engendered change. Being a veteran and a soldier, I think provided my father with a quiet confidence. Moreover, between his years in Army hospitals and the VA, he learned that just because things were done a certain way, that did not necessarily make them right.

After all, my father had the perspective of a 19-year-old soldier fumbling for money to pay for a toothbrush while laid-up in a hospital, or negotiating with a nurse to keep a record player in his room, or who was under the thumb of some self-important lieutenant worried that blinded soldiers' canes may be dinging up the hospital walls. These indignities were not easily forgotten and, in my father's case, in part fueled his persistence in helping the handicapped, and in overcoming the "that's the way it has always been done" mindset. For him, it was about serving those with vision loss, and nothing more.

Interviewing him decades later, I was constantly impressed by how my father could recall minute details about the clients he served. He knew them and their needs. The fact that he overcame many of the same challenges they were facing established my father as an inspirational figure and advocate for those with vision loss. In another words, Dad had great "street cred."

---

My father's experience as a soldier and infantryman was still a part of him and framed his outlook. In later years, he lost contact with the veterans groups he had been a part of. However, he always maintained an interest in and identification with infantrymen in later wars. It was a bond that was recognizable to me, having experienced the same thing in my own military service. He had been a soldier, a combat infantryman, and part of him always would be.

At the same time, the war was there, and it was not there. It was there in the sense that it had left my father as a person with handicaps, and not there in that as kids, it was not something we thought or talked about much with my father. It was as if World War II combat veterans had this unwritten, unstated compact that what happened over there *stayed* over there. It was okay to talk about the war at reunions or conventions, with those who had had similar experiences. But under the veterans' unsaid compact, it was not okay to talk about the war with anyone else. The horrors, the fears, and only God knows the images of things they saw, were too raw to be let loose or talked about, and were therefore kept locked away in some vault in the brain. I think with my father, it was also that he didn't want to be pitied, along with his sense that there were soldiers who had suffered worse wounds, or who had never made it back home. In short, his view was that his was not a special case.

After I'd left home, my father seemed to relive a bit of the war on at least one occasion. He listened to a book, *A Time for Trumpets*,[209] which was a history of the Battle of the Bulge. This fierce battle was fought a few weeks after Dad was wounded, and on some of the same ground in Germany and Belgium where he served. His unit, the 99th Infantry Division, played a prominent part in the battle and suffered significant casualties, including soldiers he knew. My mother said he spent a few days alone listening to the book, reliving memories he probably had shelved for decades: the wet, cold dreariness of the dense Ardennes forest, the mines and booby traps that could blow you apart or blow a limb off at any moment, the constant shelling, the guttural roar of the V-1 flying bombs overhead, the crappy food, the sleepless nights, the hatred of an enemy a few hundred yards away whose ass you wanted to kill the first chance you got, the fellow soldiers who struggled to deal with the constant tension and the fear. But, as was characteristic of my father, he probably talked about it very little.

Aside from his experience as a soldier and veteran, the anchor for my father was my mother. She had always been his anchor, and now, as his career progressed, was perhaps even more so. Mom always took an intense and genuine interest in my father's work, and in doing so, served as a terrific sounding board. This was particularly important, as at times, he instinctively kept emotions bottled up at work. As a result, he needed someone to whom he could let off a bit of frustration and who could provide a different perspective. Some of my earliest memories are of listening to my parents talk about my father's day at work as my mother cooked dinner for five kids in our tiny kitchen, while he sat on a stool in the corner: how he was handling clients who were in difficult situations, his struggle to convince the agency that people with vision loss really were capable of more than the standard expectations, the problems with infighting among those organizations dedicated to serving the blind — and the list went on.

My mother's perceptiveness about people and situations, and the fact that she was non-judgmental about people, made her a valuable confidant and counselor to my father. As a result of her grounding in Catholic social teaching, she had a strong social conscience and identified with my father's work. She was always at ease around those with handicaps, and equally at ease with people who had strong issues with my father and were not reluctant to voice them to her. In these situations, Mom's Scandinavian reserve kicked in — better to say little or nothing than to offend. As an example of her interest in my father's work and the value he placed in her counsel, she traveled on business with him when the circumstances were appropriate — at our own expense, of course.

In her role as the boss's spouse, my mother's likability helped. It was not that she didn't have opinions. She definitely did, especially about politics and religion. And it wasn't that she was timid — my father wouldn't have married her had that been the case. Rather, my mother has the gift of being able to voice an opinion, as well as knowing when not to voice an opinion.

It also helped that Mom has always been as good a listener as she is a talker, and that she genuinely identifies with people. She seems to have the knack of putting people at ease because they feel they aren't being sized up. That's Mom.

Aside from all that, Mom also knew how to throw a heck of a holiday party for agency staff. In my memory, these could be quite raucous and last until the early hours of the morning.

Being the boss's spouse easily could have been a full-time job for Mom, leaving little time to spare. Somehow, she balanced that with doing a wonderful job of raising five kids. In addition to having access to Catholic schools, sports, and all the other things that kids do, my mother's devotion to us didn't stop after we went off to college. She came to every big weekend and event at The Citadel, The Military College of South Carolina, from which three of us would graduate.

I could easily have written a book of equal length about my mother. Before the days when work-life balance become an issue for society, she did this with consummate skill. Overall, there is simply no way my father could have succeeded without her influence. Years later, my father's employees would write a ditty about his success as head of the agency, which included the line, "Part of the credit goes to Marabeth, his wife, friend and confidant throughout most of his life." The employees were partly right—a *significant* part of the credit went to Marabeth. As a partner to my father and as a mother to us, she was, and is, simply the best.

---

When I'm asked what impact my father's handicaps had on our upbringing, the easy answer is: zero, none. Our father saw to that. Even if he had not, my mother surely would not have allowed it. To me, that is the way my father always was. It simply was not a big deal.

To be sure, growing up, I knew some things about my father were different. He sometimes had to be led by the arm, he walked with a slight jerk to his steps, he didn't drive a car, and I, along with my brothers and sister, would read the newspaper to him. And he owned things that were different: a folding white cane that would snap into place when extended (that I thought was pretty cool); a book of recordings made of plastic that you could crumple up and yet still play on an old-fashioned record player; playing cards with Braille dots on them for poker and other card games; books full of the same dots, and thick beige socks for placing over his leg stumps.

From an early age, I saw his stumps. They never offended me. I never had an "eek" moment and covered my eyes. Through my adolescent lens, his stumps were a physical condition not much different from a scar or a mole. His prosthetics, like his devices to overcome his vision loss, were perhaps novelties to me. But I didn't see them as a real hindrance to my father.

I was curious about him. Apart from vague references to how he was wounded, I don't remember the war being generally talked about while I was growing up, perhaps due to the code of silence that seemed to envelop World War II veterans. Nor were there any mementos of my father's service displayed in our home. Instead, it was all kept locked away. He was in some ways an enigma to me, perhaps like other fathers who were World War II veterans. He was someone who had gone off and done something as part of a larger cause that I did not fully grasp, or even think much about, except to the extent that it involved good guys and bad guys. When a story about him and his work appeared in a local newspaper, my second grade teacher asked whether I was proud of him. The question caught me a bit off guard, because I hadn't thought about him in that way. My mumbled response was simply: "Yes."

My curiosity about my father extended to whether he really was blind. I remember playing a game of "Go Fish" with him, in which the objective was to guess the cards that the other player was holding in his or her hands, or otherwise have to pick up another card from the deck. Before he picked up his card, I remember looking at it and then guessing the card he picked up.

This may have been an instance of me being a naughty boy and cheating at cards. On the other hand, I think I was just curious as to whether my father really was blind.

I was also captivated by some of what he read. He was always an avid reader and, being blind, he received what were then referred to as "talking books" from the Library of Congress. These were old-fashioned disc records, made of plastic so they would not scratch, that he played on an equally old-fashioned record player with a turntable, needle, and speaker contained within one device. He read widely, from novels and non-fiction to various magazines. As he listened to them, sitting in a winged-back chair in our small living room, I would sit or lie on the floor nearby and listen with him. Sometimes I wasn't sure he knew I was there. At these moments, I perceived that he was in a "zone" of sorts. I didn't want to pierce that zone. Instead, I was content to be on the periphery while sharing a good read with him. Everything he listened to, I too was interested in.

Likewise, I was always fascinated when listening to my parents talk about his work. All of it interested me: the clients, the challenges, and the frustrations. Some of my earliest memories as a young child are of my mother dropping my father off in a coat and tie in front of an imposing-looking, high-rise office building. My only memory of him previous to this was when he was in a wheelchair, recovering from gallbladder surgery. Now, he worked for the government! Through the childhood lens with which I viewed my father, it all seemed so important, so consequential to me, particularly because I understood that he was helping others. As I interpreted it, if you were working for the government, you had to be an important person, doing something significant. That he soon had people working for him, and then was the head of an agency after we moved to Tallahassee, made me sure of it. My father *had* to be an important person and would be doing even bigger things.

## 25

# THE PINNACLE

Upon assuming leadership of the Bureau of Blind Services in 1974, my father's top priority was to transform the agency into a strong, more independent and visible agency to better serve the needs of people in Florida suffering from vision loss. He soon transformed this priority into twin initiatives to move the Bureau of Blind Services into the Florida Department of Education, and raise its status from an obscure bureau to a higher-level and more effective division status, a structure that at the time existed in 19 other states. This goal was aligned with Helen Keller's advocacy decades before, for a strong and independent agency in Florida to better serve the needs of the blind and visually impaired.

As early as 1929, Keller advocated for such an agency in Florida,[210] and this was indeed created that same year — only to be abolished six years later.[211] In 1941, due in part to Keller's strong advocacy, including her speech to the Florida Legislature, the creation of such an agency again became a possibility. The impact of Keller's presence in Florida was significant, as someone described by Governor Spessard Holland as "an American institution known all over the world whose influence cannot be measured because it is so boundless."[212] It took every bit of Keller's influence and trademark persistence, including her last-minute plea to Governor Holland, to get the bill creating the Florida Council for the Blind, HB 153, brought up for consideration and moved to final passage. In words that spoke of her sense of urgency and strong conviction, Keller wrote: "I implore you to pass HB 153 as a humane measure and as an act of justice to those who through no fault of their own are blind and need your help to become independent useful citizens."[213] Keller's plea worked and the bill passed. After this precarious start, the existence of the agency would again be threatened, a little over three decades later.

By 1974, the year my father assumed leadership of the Bureau of Blind Services, the organization was trapped as a sub-unit of the much larger Department of Health and Rehabilitative Services (HRS), due to reorganizations in state government. HRS was an unwieldy bureaucracy of more than 40,000 employees that had itself undergone several changes in leadership. Moreover, HRS was being considered for further reorganization, using a structure copied from the federal government. If implemented, the organizational structure would further submerge the programs for the blind and visually impaired into an unrecognizable and unaccountable maze — a maze far removed from the independent agency that Helen Keller and others had advocated for more than three decades before. HRS had become the kind of organization that sucked the air out of any real initiative. For example, as Dad later recalled, needless layers of approval were required before he could send a simple letter. In short, HRS was a bureaucratic hell.

To escape this bureaucratic Titanic before it smashed itself on the iceberg of public dissatisfaction, my father devised what became a two-step plan to move the Bureau of Blind Services to the Florida Department of Education, and later have the agency upgraded to the status of a division. Dad's initiative was more than just moving boxes around some organizational chart. Instead, it was a move that would ultimately deliver far better services to those with vision loss in Florida, unencumbered by the ineffectual edifice that was the parent organization, HRS. It was an extraordinarily bold and risky move on his part. He had been head of the agency for less than a year, and without the approval of his supervisors, was proposing a major organizational move — a move that could be met with significant opposition in the legislature, whose approval was required. If he failed, he would be forced to resign with his career shattered. Once more, my father placed his future on the line.

Dad's proposed move of the Bureau of Blind Services out

of HRS quickly created a firestorm among some in the Florida Legislature. Those legislators who had designed HRS's new organization were loath to see the neat organizational boxes they had drawn upset by a smallish, upstart agency. Alarmingly, my father was told that his proposed move would risk the loss of federal funds, which in turn would effectively gut the Bureau of Blind Services. It was a risk he was willing to take, however, to create a strong and effective agency. While he had the support of the Secretary of Education, if the move was going to happen, it was all on him. Once he made his proposal public, he alienated the leadership of his disaffected department, HRS. John F. Kennedy once said, "Victory has 100 fathers, but defeat is an orphan."[214] If my father's initiative failed, he would be just that — an orphan, and likely out of a job.

Dad, however, was politically astute, and because of his reputation among the blind and visually impaired in Florida, was able to rally support among the constituencies he served, to counter the opposition in the Florida Legislature. Skilled at building consensus and moving votes, he seemed to have an innate sense of how to present his case, and to whom. Chief among his supporters were the Blinded Veterans Association, the American Foundation for the Blind, the National Federation of the Blind and the Florida Lions. Rounding up this support among his client base significantly bolstered the effort's credibility. However, it also carried additional risks, if my father was seen as straying too far from his role as a civil servant in attempting to influence the Florida Legislature.

As his initiative to establish a truly independent agency for the blind proceeded, my father was at times roughed up in the legislature. It came to the point where my mother, who accompanied him to some of the legislative hearings, could no longer remain in the hearing room as he was grilled by legislators. During one pivotal moment, while testifying in front of a Senate committee in support of raising the status of the agency, my father was challenged by one senator, who also was the Senate President and one of the most powerful people in Florida. The senator snorted that Dad was seeking to raise the agency's stature merely because it would give him a pay raise.

Freeze frame the moment: Dad had lost both legs and his vision in serving his country, spent two years in Army hospitals relearning how to walk, read, and other basic life skills, and worked relentlessly for those with vision loss in Florida. Now he was being treated like a self-interested bureaucrat—as if it were all about him. Few things get under my father's skin—by having his integrity questioned is one of them.

He kept his composure. His response to the senator's challenge was: "I'm happy to give up any pay raise, and in fact, you can even write it into the bill." It was a bold statement, particularly as the bill raising the agency's status was being considered before a committee of five, where Dad needed three votes. To convince one senator and get his vote, he canvassed the support of the Blinded Veterans Association and the Veterans Administration. The second vote came from another senator on the committee who was a strong supporter. The third and deciding vote surprisingly came from the Senate President whom my father had essentially told to take his pay raise and shove it. Apparently, the senator respected blunt feedback. It was another pivotal moment: by a 3-2 vote, the bill moved out of committee.

Even then, Dad was not done. By custom, each senator had two or three bills they could post for consideration by the full Senate in the crunch time usually associated with the end of a legislative session. For whatever reason, the sponsoring senator in this case decided the agency for the blind was not a top priority, and did not post the bill. This meant he was effectively killing it. Once again, my father's persistence kicked in. This time, he boldly interrupted a meeting the senator was in, much to the senator's displeasure, to politely insist the bill be posted. It was.

Persistence wasn't the only reason for Dad's success in moving the legislation forward. Throughout these tussles, he was able to garner support from his most important source: his clients. Eventually, he was successful in transferring the Bureau of Blind Services into the Florida Department of Education, as of April 1,

1976, and in having it upgraded to the status of a division the following year. It was quite an accomplishment, my father having been head of the agency for only two years. And, more than 45 years after Helen Keller first advocated for the establishment of an independent state agency in Florida to serve those with vision loss, my father fully accomplished that goal.

Dad's initiative to elevate the status of the Florida Division of Blind Services was part of its transformation into one of the leading and most effective agencies of its kind in the United States. Indeed, the Division of Blind Services became known as the nation's flagship state agency for serving the blind and visually impaired, and drew visitors from as far away as New Zealand to learn more about its practices. In recognition of this, my father was elected president of the American Association of Workers for the Blind, and was honored by the National Accreditation Council for Agencies Serving the Blind and Visually Handicapped. For this latter recognition, he received a congratulatory letter from President Ronald Reagan, stating, "Your selfless efforts to help others epitomize the finest qualities of the human spirit. The source of America's greatness rests with individuals like you who generously give of themselves to make others happy. That's a shining example for all of us."[215]

Dad was also called to testify before Congress on several occasions, in support of programs that benefitted the elderly blind, blind children, and blind veterans. In addition, he continued to have success in the Florida Legislature through efforts to extend tax credits to blind veterans, and to allow guide dogs for the blind to have unimpeded access to restaurants and hotels.

Running the newly designated Division of Blind Services was not just a lot of feel-good. It meant some hard dealing and bringing together disparate groups with different ideas about how to serve those with vision loss, as well as bridging conflicts between diverse personalities. An example of this was when my father was presented with the idea of establishing a center to train the multi-handicapped blind—those with handicaps in addition to being blind—in life skills, so they could manage at home. Referring to my father's predecessor, Millard Conklin, a well-known civic leader whose goal it was to establish such a center, told Dad that he couldn't work with "that son of a bitch."

The multi-handicapped blind were faced with the greatest challenges in developing life skills. Establishing a training center focused on their needs had been a dream for several years in Florida, given its relatively large population of people with vision loss. In pressing forward with the initiative to co-found the center for the multi-handicapped blind, Dad once again encountered opposition within his agency. This time it came from his senior staff, who didn't think such a center was needed. In the end, Conklin and Dad got it done. In 1979, they co-founded the Conklin Center as a public-private partnership, in Daytona Beach, Florida. The center provides a campus-like setting for training the multi-handicapped blind to achieve independent living.

For the multi-handicapped, nothing comes easy. All those daily functions we take for granted—taking a shower, getting dressed in the morning, cooking a meal—present challenges to them. Prior to the advent of facilities like the Conklin Center, independent living was largely not an option for those with multi-handicaps, their only real option being either life with a caregiver, or institutionalization.

Recognizing this need, the Conklin Center became the first non-profit, human services agency in the nation dedicated to training adults with vision loss and an additional disability, to be able to find employment and live independently. Being multi-handicapped himself, my father perhaps recognized this need more than some, including those on his own staff who resisted the idea. With his characteristic persistence, he nonetheless had pressed ahead in co-founding the center.

Today the Conklin Center continues its independent-living training functions at its nine-acre campus in Daytona Beach. In recognition of my father's support, the center dedicated a vocational wing, Wedewer Hall, in 1986.

Similarly, Dad partnered with other strong personalities to establish 16 regional centers throughout Florida to serve those with vision loss, through training and other programs, as part of another series of public and private partnerships. This kind of give-and-take and dealing extended to the Florida Legislature, where even after his earlier battles, my father faced new challenges in having to fight for his budget each year. Such was the case when the issue of pensions for some of his employees came up again in a Senate budget hearing. Dad expressed his reluctance at having to address what was seemingly an annual issue. The swift response, from the interested senator and erstwhile friend: "Fuck off." Don Wedewer, friend or not, blinded veteran or not, you are going to have to address the pension issue again.

In retrospect, even with all the bureaucratic haggling, running the agency was in a sense comparatively easy for my father. His war and hospital experiences certainly placed things in context. The move of the Bureau of Blind Services and the subsequent upgrade in its status laid the foundation for providing better services for people with vision loss. Today, the Division of Blind Services remains a part of the Florida Department of Education and provides services to tens of thousands of people with vision loss in Florida.

For all the tussles in the Florida Legislature, and challenges and frustrations associated with running a large agency, there were occasional, poignant moments. One came in May 1985, when my father appeared on the floor of the Florida Senate with Jewish victims of the Nazi Holocaust. Their appearance coincided with the passage of a resolution in the Florida Senate designating "Days of Remembrance" for Holocaust victims.[216] Dad represented the liberators of the death camps, while victims were represented by a couple from Poland who lost family members, including their daughter, to the Nazi's slaughter.[217] In this brief moment, someone who gave it all was reunited with people who had suffered at the hands of an evil ideology capable of monstrous, incomprehensible crimes. My father was there to represent those who were not, including buddies and fellow soldiers—Chambliss, Venter, Klewing, and others who were shot, frozen to death, or blown apart. He had some reticence about attending the ceremony, probably because he made it and many did not. In his characteristic fashion, he felt others were more deserving. It was one of the few occasions on which there was a public connection between my father and the events of decades before. It was a moment such as only the passage of time permits, when everything else was placed in perspective.

Overall, my father had that trait of being able to undertake large projects or difficult problems, break them into solvable, component parts, and then develop a solution. For each issue, Dad could always envision the long-term goal for what he wanted to do for those with vision loss—aided by his own experience as a veteran and someone who was blind—and then articulate that goal in ways that others could understand and accept. In short, Dad had the gift of leadership that was ideally suited for his field.

At the same time, his outlook and leadership style in some ways emulated that of one of his political heroes and his college graduation speaker from many years before, President Harry Truman. As an agency head and leader, Dad had those Trumanesque qualities of plain speaking and bold decision-making, combined with an everyperson demeanor that connected with people and, most importantly, with his clients. Dad also seemed to have an intuitive sense of what those who were blind or visually impaired aspired to, along with the practical skills to provide them with the tools to reach those aspirations. Although as a civil servant he did not hold an elective public office, he effectively became the voice of people with vision loss in Florida. It is probably rare that a civil servant would achieve such a status, but that is what he did, because of his tireless advocacy and willingness to be bold, and perhaps aided by the respect his wartime service commanded.

Also like Truman, my father has a deep sense of integrity and a sense of the trust placed in public servants. While believing in the provision of government services to those in need, he also believes in frugality and abhors government waste. That is the way he ran his agency. I remember him often saying that government does not on its own create wealth, hence, every dollar his agency received from taxpayers that could otherwise be used to create wealth was going to be spent in a way that maximized client service and mission accomplishment. At times, Dad's frugality got under the skin of a few employees, who complained about being harangued over excessive travel expenses. My father had a tin ear for such complaints. His invariable response: deal with it and move on.

As demanding a boss as my father could be, he was adored by his employees throughout the years. Many were young and idealistic, and would follow him anywhere. Their respect and adoration was perhaps best captured in their nomination of him for a "Boss of the Year" award:

> "His warmth, good humor and his concern for those around him is unique and special. He has a deep concern for the well being of clients and fellow staff members. He respects their opinions, their feelings and shows much sensitivity towards others. Under extreme pressure, he still maintains poise and cheerfulness—never demonstrating irritation or ill feeling. His leadership is by example rather than by authority. Those who work with and for him innately want to give their very best to their job ... He is a wonderful person who gives inspiration every day."[218]

Perhaps small recognition, but it was emblematic of the kind of respect my father gained through example.

The employees' reverence for my father was well-founded, because he had a gift for recognizing those who were self-starters. He exercised a leadership style that focused on providing these employees with the tools and authority to better do their jobs. Some have called it leadership by subservience.

Dad's style of leadership had a particular impact on improving the career prospects of women who worked in the division, who were traditionally confined to lower-level jobs. Through his opening up of a master's degree program in vocational rehabilitation to social workers in the agency, many of whom were women, they were able to take advantage of an opportunity that would propel their careers. Some, such as Priscilla Rogers, would go on to head other agencies serving the blind.

Another example of his promotion of the role of women was Bobbie Hammond-Wheeler, who joined the agency in 1957 as a medical counselor for the elderly. At that time, the preferred gender for the position was stipulated as male. Hence, as a condition for her employment, Wheeler-Hammond had to write a master's degree-grade paper on why a woman could perform the job as well as a man.[219] Today, it seems utterly bizarre. In any case, Wheeler-Hammond was an absolute dynamo and a few years later had over 500 clients.[220] Wheeler-Hammond was particularly good with kids, and later undertook coordination of the program at Camp Achievement, an initiative designed for pre-school blind children and their parents. She also started a group for the parents of blind children. At Wheeler-Hammond's retirement, after 33 years of service, Dad quipped that he was "pleased to have worked for Bobbie Wheeler-Hammond."[221]

---

In 1989, after serving those who were blind and visually impaired in Florida for approximately 25 years, my father retired. During that time, Florida became a very different place for those suffering from vision loss, due in significant measure to Dad's leadership. More than 120,000 blind and visually impaired persons were registered to receive services during his 15-year tenure, compared to 86,000 registered during the previous 32 years.[222] There were now 16 new regional centers to serve people with vision loss.[223] Twelve new districts were established within the division to better serve the blind and visually impaired at the local level.[224] Library services to people with vision loss were significantly expanded. Services to the elderly blind were expanded. Financial assistance was provided to blind students to attend the finest colleges and universities. A center for the multi-handicapped blind was established. Gifted employees, particularly women, were given new opportunities to serve those with vision loss, and the blind and visually impaired had a firmly established agency to better serve their needs. Moreover, my father's influence extended nationally as his initiatives and reforms were recognized by other state agencies serving the blind and visually impaired.

At Dad's retirement, his employees wrote a riff about his time at the agency, which included the passage:

> "Around here, he's admired
>
> as a co-worker and a friend,
>
> Competent but caring
>
> a much desired blend.
>
> Multiple handicaps
>
> have never deterred,
>
> From Don there's seldom
>
> a discouraging word.
>
> With endless courage
>
> he epitomizes the best,
>
> and has tackled every hurdle
>
> with incredible zest."[225]

---

In 1990, Dad was awarded the Migel Medal—the highest honor in the blindness field—which is bestowed by the American Foundation for the Blind.[226] The foundation is one of the nation's premier organizations that supports people with vision loss and their families. Named after a philanthropist who wanted to help the large number of veterans blinded during World War I, the Migel Medal was a particularly fitting award for my father.[227] Previous awardees included several U.S. senators and the industrialist Henry Ford.[228]

Now, it was Dad's turn for recognition. A passage in the award program said it all:

> "Mr. Wedewer and Mr. Claude [the other awardee] have dedicated much of their adult lives to helping improve the quality of life for blind and visually impaired people. Through dedication and much hard work, they have succeeded admirably."[229]

Similarly, a letter my father received from President George H.W. Bush and Barbara Bush stated, "Through their many years of dedicated leadership and hard work, Mr. Wedewer and Mr. Claude have earned this high honor and respect and gratitude it represents. Their efforts to help Americans with visual disabilities lead fuller, more independent, and more productive lives stands as a wonderful example of the American spirit of service to others ..."[230]

For 40 years, Helen Keller, the most famous ambassador of the American Foundation for the Blind, championed the cause of people with vision loss. Now, in receiving the Migel Medal, my father received the organization's highest award—44 years after briefly connecting with Keller during an inspirational meeting. One was a groundbreaking woman and perhaps the most influential person with vision loss in the world, and the other, a 20-year-old wounded veteran with an uncertain future. Now, their paths crossed a final time.

## 26

## FINAL CALLING

THE MIGEL MEDAL WAS A fitting bookend to Dad's career in public service and his work on behalf of people with vision loss. Yet, he still had more to do. In 1994, he was appointed by President Bill Clinton to the Committee for Purchase from People Who Are Blind or Severely Disabled.[231] The primary mission of the committee is increasing employment and training opportunities to help prepare these workers for competitive employment.[232] The committee determines fair market prices for commodities and services offered for sale to the federal government by non-profit agencies employing persons who are blind or have other severe disabilities.[233] The committee also assists federal agencies to expand procurement from participating organizations.[234]

In addition to the presidential appointment, my father continued his public service in other areas. Around the same time, he was appointed by Florida Governor Lawton Chiles to the Florida State Commission on Transportation for the Disadvantaged. The commission is charged with overseeing the distribution of funds to taxi, van, and bus services or Community Transportation Coordinators for the transportation of the poor, the disabled, children, and the elderly in Florida's 67 counties.[235] Dad served for nine years on the commission and four years as its chair. In doing so, he oversaw services to more than 630,000 passengers annually embarking on more than 32 million trips and involving $180 million in operating expenses.[236] Even in what was presumably an uncontroversial role suited for semi-retirement, my father found himself in the middle of fiscal battles, as various interests in the transportation industry sought a greater slice of the lucrative transportation budget. These interests were aggressive in doing so, and at one point were behind a move to add 10 new members to the commission's membership to ensure they received a greater take of the budget.[237]

Although the title came with its frustrations, my father's chairmanship of the transportation committee for the disadvantaged positioned him for the final achievement of his career. After much lobbying and effort, he persuaded the Florida Legislature to pass a bill that increased the funds available for transportation for the disadvantaged and disabled by providing a larger share of license plate revenues. For the disadvantaged and disabled, transportation to school, job training, or to obtain medical services was more than point A to point B. It was a lifeline. In lobbying individual legislators to support the bill, Dad literally wore his stumps red from walking the halls of the Florida capitol with his characteristic persistence. The effort was worth it. Through his efforts, an additional $10 million per year was allocated to support the transportation of those in need.

What drove my father, however late in life, to vigorously pursue this endeavor was, at least in part, his deep commitment to public service. How much his commitment was mixed with his desire to overcome the perceived barriers to those with handicaps, or worse, unwanted pity from others, I do not fully know, because he has always been that person my mother described as living in his head. What I do know, though, is that whether as a 19-year-old soldier lying horribly wounded in a hospital bed, with seemingly not much of a future, or in the twilight years of his public service, my father never accepted that he would be inconsequential to society. A society that, while appreciating his service, was not always fully prepared to embrace the fact that someone with handicaps could still make a significant contribution for the greater good.

Perhaps that was the lesson my father learned long ago, while a patient at Bushnell Army Hospital, from his mentor Joe Miller, who called him "the bravest guy I have ever seen." Joe Miller who, through deeds more than words, simply refused to accept that a person with handicaps, in his case a double amputee at age

12, could not make a difference. Joe took his belief straight to the top — literally to the president.

As far as I can determine, no monument was ever erected to Joe Miller. Nor was there any other formal recognition of him. It doesn't matter. Perhaps the real monument to Joe Miller is the lives in which he made a difference, and in turn, the positive impact those who Joe helped, such as my father, were able to make in others' lives. In my father's case, it would be tens of thousands of lives. Perhaps Joe sensed something special about my father decades before. I do not know for sure. What I do know, though, is that my father truly lived up to being the bravest guy Joe Miller had ever seen.

# EPILOGUE

In 2000, I visited the American Military Cemetery at Henri-Chapelle in Belgium, which serves as the final resting place for 7,992 Americans killed in the European theater during World War II. It is located on a picturesque plateau overlooking a valley dotted with farms. At the entrance is an archway, and beyond it the graves, arrayed in neat rows bordered by equally well-kept grass. I went there to perhaps connect with part of my father's past, by understanding and appreciating to a greater degree the sacrifices of his fellow soldiers. Before going, I wasn't sure whether any soldiers in my father's unit, the 99th Infantry Division, were buried at the Henri-Chapelle cemetery. I soon learned. In Row 1, I counted three dead from the 99th. By Row 10, I was up to at least 13. I did not finish my count, because I had the uncomfortable sense this was almost my father's fate. And, even knowing the history of World War II and its reputation as being a "Good War" free of moral ambiguities, I felt the pressure of an inescapable question: what the hell were these young Americans doing here?

My visit to Henri-Chapelle and other sites also brought into stark view the unimaginable level of brutality and killing that was World War II. It was a far darker reality than that portrayed in the sanitized World War II movies and television shows I had been exposed to growing up, in which the good guys never bled when they got shot, and there was rarely a whiff of the stupidity or ineptness that characterized many of the decisions that led to American casualties. Perhaps, as was the case with many World War II veterans, this darker reality of the war was the one that in my father's case, remained largely locked away.

As I departed the Henri-Chapelle cemetery, I encountered the Belgian cemetery custodian. Even before I spoke, she identified me as a "war baby" coming to learn more about his parents. She then sighed wistfully and said she saw a lot of us there. And, with the wars in Afghanistan and Iraq, I suspect that, sadly, there will be more like me visiting cemeteries for a long time to come. I hope these future generations will have the opportunity that I had to connect in some tangible way with their family's past.

More recently, I visited my father's birthplace in Dyersville, Iowa, with my son Ben. It's a place I had no memory of, having last visited as a one-year-old. While standing in the freezing rain over the grave of my grandfather, also named Ben Wedewer, I sensed I had come full circle in an experience that started in Pennsylvania at a 99th Infantry Division reunion, and led to drives around Texas, and then to Liège, Belgium, the Ardennes Forest, the American cemeteries at Henri-Chapelle and Neuville-en-Condroz in Belgium, the Hürtgen Forest in Germany, and then back to Valley Forge, Pennsylvania, the National Archives in College Park, Maryland, former Army bases in Texas, and the University of Missouri in Columbia. My 15-year journey—interrupted by my going to law school at night—uncovered a previously obscure truth and answered a subconscious question I did not know that I had asked.

---

Framed in my office is a yellowing newspaper clipping entitled "In Public Service." In a few sentences it announces my father's appointment by President Bill Clinton to the Committee for Purchase from People Who Are Blind or Severely Disabled. My mother sent me the clipping years ago. Since then it has made several military and office moves, always occupying a place of prominence on a shelf or desk. I never thought much about why I kept the framed clipping close, or instead, whether it was just another fading office trinket that had lost its meaning a long time ago.

Through writing about my father, though, I learned that while at times he seemed a somewhat distant, enigmatic figure to me, he was in fact always close. Far more than I previously recognized, he positively influenced many decisions I made, as well as my outlook on life. At times it was because of what he *didn't* say. Such was the case when I entered the military. Given his experience with war, people expressed surprise that my father allowed me and one of my older brothers to serve, or at least never counseled against it. Certainly in their view, he would have been embittered by his experience. He was not. There was never a trace of bitterness from my father. That wasn't his way. Now, two of his grandsons serve this country in uniform.

My father's influence permeated every other major decision I made, including entering public service after retiring from the military. Unconsciously, perhaps like many sons, I was trying to live up to my father's example and perceived expectations. I will never meet those, of course—what son ever really ever does, when such expectations are self-imposed? But, I found you become better in the process of trying.

Overall, in writing about my father, I learned about someone I did not know well, and the great extent to which he influenced me. Indeed, his is an influence I take to work every day. And now, that small, innocuous newspaper clipping is a little more prominent on my desk.

I won't describe my father's wounding, recovery, and ultimate success as "remarkable," because that is not a characterization he likes. Rather, it is a story of a private man with granite determination, perseverance, and an innate sense of optimism, interwoven with the environment and institutions of his youth. In that sense, my father's life is the product of the influences that combined to make up his journey. Whatever one attributes the success of that journey to, it can nevertheless serve as an example for us all.

My father's life has also taught me that in one's life, events can take unexpected turns for the better, only if you let them. He did, and for that, I will be forever grateful.

# ACKNOWLEDGEMENTS

I would like to thank Major Kenneth J. Koyle, U.S. Army, of the U.S. Army Medical Department Office of Medical History, for his invaluable assistance in locating the archives of the 15th General Hospital and recreating the events of that terrible morning in Liège.

The staff of the National Archives in College Park, Maryland, were wonderfully helpful in pulling together the after-action reports of the 99th Infantry Division and its various components.

SFC Linda R. Surber of the Texas Army National Guard, a member of the Camp Maxey Training Center garrison, was of great assistance in opening the archives at the camp during my visit there. The custodian of the Fort Wolters "motor pool" was equally helpful during my impromptu visit, and provided a very informative tour of the old base.

I would like to thank the 99th Infantry Division Association for serving as such wonderful hosts during the division reunion.

Dr. Gary Cox of the University of Missouri archives and his staff were extraordinarily generous with their time and helpful suggestions during my visit there. They were wonderful hosts as well.

I would also like to thank Andrea Carter, from the University of Northern Utah, for her gracious assistance in allowing me access to her Master's thesis regarding the history of Bushnell General Military Hospital. It is a terrific paper and was of great help. I would also like to thank her advisor, Dr. David Rich Lewis of the University of Northern Utah.

Sam Rushay, a supervisory archivist at the Harry S. Truman Library in Independence, Missouri, was very helpful in providing access to the president's commencement address at the University of Missouri.

Equally helpful was the National Park Service in providing me with a guided tour of the Truman home in Independence.

Dr. Dan Mortensen, Ph.D., at the University of Valley Forge, was of enormous assistance in giving me access to his work regarding the history of the Valley Forge Army General Hospital, as well as providing me with a very informative tour of the site, now the University of Valley Forge.

I would like to thank Father Richard Kruse of the Basilica of St. Francis Xavier in Dyersville, Iowa, who graciously took time to give me a tour as well as a visit to the Catholic gravesite outside of town. Equally helpful were the people of Dyersville, who were every bit as hospitable as I thought they would be during my visit there.

Helen Selsdon at the American Foundation for the Blind was wonderfully helpful in providing information and photos from the Helen Keller archives, and reading portions of the manuscript.

The Florida Division of Blind Services and the Florida Library for the Blind were of great assistance in providing a history of services to those with vision loss in Florida.

I would like to thank the people of Belgium, and in particular the people of Liège. To a person, they were extraordinarily helpful and polite, in pointing me in the right direction, despite my complete lack of language skills. The American Battle Monuments Commission staff at the American Military Cemeteries at Henri-Chapelle and the Ardennes do a wonderful job of maintaining very moving sites, and were helpful in orienting me.

Nancy and Bill Feld were great in sharing memories, papers, and photos of my father.

Professor Dave Belz at Loyola University Maryland provided terrific editing of my draft manuscript.

My editor, Sue Copsey, who from far-off New Zealand did an equally terrific job of condensing and focusing my work.

The incredibly talented Glendon Haddix and his team of

professionals at Streetlight Graphics for their work on the cover design and formatting.

Finally, I would like to thank my mother and father for submitting to seemingly unending interviews and questions for over a decade. For my father, these interviews at times brought up some suppressed and painful memories that he much preferred to forget, but nonetheless shared. Similarly, I would like to thank my wonderful wife, Robin, and son, Ben, who through their encouragement, reading the draft manuscript, and most important, just being who they are, provided the inspiration to finish this book.

# NOTES

## Prologue

1. Benjamin King and Timothy J. Kutta, *Impact: The History of Germany's V-Weapons in World War II* (New York: Sarpedon, 1998).

2. Muriel Phillips Engelman, interview US Army Nurse at Battle of the Bulge – WWII.mov, https://www.youtube.com/watch?v=2PO2MAktnEw.

3. King and Kutta, *Impact: The History of Germany's V-Weapons In World War II*, 285.

4. U.S. Army, 15th General Hospital, "Semi-Annual History 15th General Hospital, 1 January 1945 –30 June 1945."

5. "Fayembois (Jupille) and the 16th General Hospital" (written by Second Lieutenant Muriel Phillips Engelman), Battle of The Bulge Memories, last updated June 28, 2013, http://www.battleofthebulgememories.be/en/stories/us-army/365-fayembois-jupille-and-the-16th-general-hospital.html. For a comparable account, see "Fayembois (Jupille) and the 16th General Hospital" (1st Lt Muriel Phillips Engelman, 16th General Hospital), Office de Promotion de Tourisme Wallonie-Bruxelles, accessed January 3, 2015. http://www.criba.be/fr/stories/detail/fayembois-jupille-and-the-16th-general-hospital-257-1.

Photographs of where the V-1 hit can be found at http://ihm.nlm.nih.gov.

6. Newspaper clipping, Donald H. Wedewer Papers, in the author's possession.

7. "World War II Burials and Memorializations," American Battle Monuments Commission, accessed January 3, 2015, http://www.abmc.gov/node/1274. For corroboration of this figure, see "By the Numbers: The U.S. Military," National World War II Museum, accessed January 4, 2015, http://www.nationalww2museum.org/learn/education/for-students/ww2-history/ww2-by-the-numbers/us-military.html.

8. "By the Numbers: The U.S. Military," National World War II Museum, accessed January 4, 2015, http://www.nationalww2museum.org/learn/education/for-students/ww2-history/ww2-by-the-numbers/us-military.html.

9. "Honor List of World War II Dead and Missing Dubuque County, Iowa," War Department (available through the National Archives and Records Administration), accessed January 3, 2015, https://www.archives.gov/research/military/ww2/army-casualties/iowa.html.

10. *Dyersville, Iowa Centennial Official History and Program July 9–15, 1972*, Dyersville Area Centennial Corporation.

## Chapter 1 Beginnings

11. *Dyersville, Iowa Centennial Official History and Program July 9–15, 1972*, Dyersville Area Centennial Corporation.

12. *Field of Dreams*. Directed by Phil Alden Robinson. 1989. Universal City, CA: Universal Studios. Anniversary Edition, DVD.

13. Basilica of St. Francis Xavier, accessed March 1, 2016, http://xavierbasilica.com.

14. *Dyersville, Iowa Centennial Official History and Program July 9–15, 1972*, Dyersville Area Centennial Corporation

15. Ibid.

16. Ibid.

## Chapter 2 The War

17. Herodatus, *The Histories* (Digireads.com Publishing, 2009).

18. *Dyersville, Iowa Centennial Official History and Program July 9-15, 1972*, Dyersville Area Centennial Corporation.

19. Ibid.

20. "Reichstag Speech by Adolph Hitler, January 30, 1939," United States Holocaust Memorial Museum, http://www.ushmm.org/learn/timeline-of-events/1939-1941/hitler-speech-to-german-parliament.

21. "Gassing Operations," United States Holocaust Memorial Museum, last updated August 18, 2015, http://www.ushmm.org/wlc/en/article.php?ModuleId=10005220.

22. "Prime Minister Winston Churchill, Broadcast Regarding His Meeting With Roosevelt," August 24, 1941. Online by the Jewish Virtual Library, http://www.jewishvirtuallibrary.org/jsource/ww2/churchill082441.html.

23. Office of Strategic Services Research and Analysis Branch, *The Greater East Asia Co-Prosperity Sphere*, accessed September 7, 2015, http://www.foia.cia.gov/sites/default/files/document_conversions/89801/DOC_0000710366.pdf.

24. Iris Chang, *The Rape of Nanking* (New York: Basic Books 2011).

25. Franklin D. Roosevelt, "Radio Address Announcing an Unlimited National Emergency," May 27, 1941. Online by Gerhard Peters and John T. Woolley, The American Presidency Project, University of California Santa Barbara, http://www.presidency.ucsb.edu/ws/?pid=16120.

26. Ibid.

27. "World War II Valor In the Pacific, People," U.S. National Park Service, accessed January 2, 2015, http://www.nps.gov/nr/twhp/wwwlps/lessons/18arizona/18charts1.htm.

28. "World War II Valor In the Pacific, History and Culture," U.S. National Park Service, accessed January 2, 2015, http://www.nps.gov/valr/historyculture/index.htm. The U.S. National Park Service maintains the USS *Arizona* memorial.

29. Whether these words were actually said by Admiral Yamamato, the Japanese commander, has been widely debated. They appear in two films about the attack on Pearl Harbor, but their authenticity has not been verified. I used them because they appear to at least capture the sentiment of the admiral.

30. "Pearl Harbor Raid, 7 December 1941 Raid Aftermath," U.S. Naval History & Heritage Command, accessed January 5, 2015, http://www.history.navy.mil/our-collections/photography/wars-and-events/world-war-ii/pearl-harbor-raid/raid-aftermath.html.

31. U.S. Army, *Camp Wolters, Infantry Replacement Training Center Guide*, accessed January 2, 2015, http://www.fortwolters.com/Camp%20Wolters%20Guide%20Gallery/index.htm.

32. Donald H. Wedewer, His Service Record, in the author's possession.

33. U.S. Army Historical Section, *Army Ground Forces Study No. 7, Provision of Enlisted Replacements, Functional of the Replacement System In 1942*, last updated October 17, 2005, http://www.history.army.mil/books/agf/AGF007/ch03.htm.

34. U.S. Army, Infantry Replacement Training Center, *IRTC I am a Doughboy*, 5, accessed January 2, 2015, http://www.fortwolters.com/IRTC%20-%20Doughboy%20Gallery/index.htm.

35. Donald H. Wedewer, His Service Record, in the author's possession.

36. "George S. Patton Jr. Quotes," Goodreads, http://www.goodreads.com/author/quotes/370054.George_S_Patton_Jr_.

37. U.S. Army Signal Corps, *Kill or Be Killed*, War Department Training Film, T.F. 21 1024, 1943, posted by Jeff Quitney on February 26, 2012, https://www.youtube.com/watch?v=C4_VqgqBk7E.

38. U.S. Army, *Camp Wolters Infantry Replacement Training Center Guide*, accessed January 2, 2015, http://www.fortwolters.com/Camp%20Wolters%20Guide%20Gallery/index.htm.

39. U.S. Army Service Forces Signal Corps, Rifle U.S. Cal. 30 M1, War Department Training Film T.F.9 1172, 1943, posted by Arms Control Center on July 29, 2010, https://www.youtube.com/watch?v=lo0NLKAvmDM.

40. "History of the Expert Infantryman Badge," U.S. Army Maneuver Center of Excellence, accessed January 3, 2015, http://www.benning.army.mil/infantry/eib/history.html. Further information regarding the first recipient of the Expert Infantryman Badge can be found in: PFC Lorie Goodrow, "Walter Bull," *Soldiers*, May 1982, http://www.scribd.com/doc/47935500/PFC-Walter-Bull-The-First-Expert-Infantryman.

41. Daniel K. Gibran, *The 92nd Infantry Division and the Italian Campaign in World War II* (Jefferson, North Carolina: McFarland & Company, Inc., 2001), 94. Additional information regarding discrimination in Mineral Wells can be found in: Louie Robinson, "The Return of a Native Writer Views Changes of Texas Birthplace," *Ebony*, August 1971, http://books.google.com/books?id=DNwDAAAAMBAJ&pg=PA120&lpg=PA120&dq=mineral+wells+texas+and+1971+ebony+article&source=bl&ots=p8TqlCiwTm&sig=I-2mOkerrb97UYZ41ydnOG5tm8E&hl=en&sa=X&ei=Qij_Tt6VM4nY0QH5yP2WAg&sqi=2&ved=0CCYQ6AEwAg#v=onepage&q&f=false.

42. U.S. Army, Infantry Replacement Training Center, *IRTC I am a Doughboy*, 61, accessed January 2, 2015, http://www.fortwolters.com/IRTC%20-%20Doughboy%20Gallery/index.htm.

## Chapter 3 The 99th

43. Orientation Branch, Information and Education Division, European Theater of Operations, United States Army, *Battle Babies: The Story of the 99th Infantry Division*, accessed January 3, 2015, http://www.lonesentry.com/gi_stories_booklets/99thinfantry/. This booklet is one of the series of GI stories published by the Stars & Stripes in Paris in 1944–1945.

44. European Theater of Operations, Divisions, Office of the Theater Historian, Paris, France, *Order of Battle of the United States Army World War II, European Theater of Operations*, December 1945, accessed December 13, 2014, http://www.history.army.mil/documents/ETO-OB/99ID-ETO.htm.

45. Joseph Heller, *Catch-22* (1961; repr.,50th Anniversary Edition, New York: Simon & Schuster, 2011).

46. "Holocaust Encyclopedia, The 99th Infantry Division," United States Holocaust Memorial Museum, last updated June 20, 2014, http://www.ushmm.org/wlc/en/article.php?ModuleId=10006153.

47. "Holocaust Encyclopedia, Mühldorf," United States Holocaust Memorial Museum, last updated June 20, 2014, http://www.ushmm.org/wlc/en/article.php?ModuleId=10006172.

48. "Holocaust Encyclopedia, The 99th Infantry Division," United States Holocaust Memorial Museum, last updated June 20, 2014, http://www.ushmm.org/wlc/en/article.php?ModuleId=10006153.

49. "Two Held In Crash Death Near Dubuque Waterloo Pair Jailed

For Investigation, Whiskey Is Sought," *Waterloo Daily Courier* (Waterloo, IA), April 12, 1944.

## Chapter 4 Across the Atlantic

50. "United States Maritime Commission C3 Type Ships," United States Merchant Marine.org, accessed January 3, 2015, http://www.usmm.org/c3ships.html. To view a profile of the USAT *Exchequer*, see "Outboard Profiles of Maritime Commission Vessels The C3 Cargo Ship, Sub-Designs and Conversions," U.S. Maritime Commission, accessed January 3, 2015, http://drawings.usmaritimecommission.de/drawings_c3.htm.

51. "CU Convoy Series," Arnold Hague Convoy Database, accessed January 3, 2015, http://www.convoyweb.org.uk/cu/index.html.

52. Douglas M. McLean, "The Battle of Convoy BX-141," *Northern Mariner 3*, no. 4 (1993): 19-35, accessed January 3, 2015, http://www.cnrs-scrn.org/northern_mariner/vol03/tnm_3_4_19-35.pdf. For additional details regarding the attack on Convoy BX-141, see "Ships hit from Convoy BX-141," Uboat.net, accessed January 3, 2015, http://uboat.net/ops/convoys/convoys.php?convoy=BX-141.

53. McLean, "The Battle of Convoy BX-141," 23-32.

54. Ibid.

55. "CU Convoy Series," Arnold Hague Convoy Database, accessed January 3, 2015, http://www.convoyweb.org.uk/cu/index.html. To view further information regarding the CU series convoys, see "CU Convoys – 1943-1945," Warsailors.com, accessed January 3, 2015, http://www.warsailors.com/convoys/cuconvoys.html.

56. "CU Convoy Series," Arnold Hague Convoy Database, accessed January 3, 2015, http://www.convoyweb.org.uk/cu/index.html.

57. "Index to Ship Histories – Dictionary of American Naval

Fighting Ships," U.S. Naval History & Heritage Command, accessed January 3, 2015, http://www.history.navy.mil/research/histories/ship-histories/danfs.html.

58. "USAT Dorchester Files," U.S. Navy Armed Guard.com, accessed December 14, 2014, http://www.armed-guard.com/dork.html.

59. Sam Jenkins, interview, The Digital Collections of the National World War II Museum, http://ww2online.org/view/sam-jenkins/segment-2.

60. Ibid.

## Chapter 5 England

61. King and Kutta, *Impact: The History of Germany's V-Weapons In World War II*, 258.

62. Ibid., 258-259.

63. Ibid., 259.

## Chapter 6 To the Front Lines

64. "A History of USS LST-325, 1942-2001," The USS LST Ship Memorial, accessed December 15, 2014, http://www.1stmemorial.org/pages/history.html. For additional information regarding LSTs, see "LST History," LST 393, accessed December 15, 2014, http://www.lst393.org/history/lst-general.html.

65. U.S. Army Medical Department, Office of Medical History, "Official History Medical Department of the United States Army in World War II, Cold Injury, Ground Type, Chapter VII European Theater of Operations," 142, accessed December 20, 2014, http://history.amedd.army.mil/booksdocs/wwii/ColdInjury/Chapter07.htm.

66. Ibid.

67. PFC James L. Haseltine, ed. *From Battle Babies to Vets: The Combat History of the 394th Infantry Regiment.* n.p., 3.

68. Headquarters 394th Infantry, "History of the 394th Infantry Regiment, 99th Infantry Division, 1 January 1944 through 31 December 1944," 14.

69. U.S. Army Medical Department, Office of Medical History, "History of the Medical Department of the United States Army, World War II, Cold Injury, Ground Type, Chapter VII: European Theater of Operations," accessed December 20, 2014, http://history.amedd.army.mil/booksdocs/wwii/ColdInjury/Chapter07.htm.

70. Ibid.

71. Ibid.

72. Ibid.

73. Ibid.

74. PFC James L. Haseltine, ed., *From Battle Babies to Vets: The Combat History of the 394th Infantry Regiment.* n.p., 4.

75. Ibid., 5.

76. Ibid., 4.

77. "Hungry History," The History Channel, accessed January 4, 2015, http://www.history.com/news/hungry-history/d-day-rations-how-chocolate-helped-win-the-war.

78. PFC James L. Haseltine ed., *From Battle Babies to Vets: The Combat History of the 394th Infantry Regiment*, n.p., p. 3.

79. U.S. Government, War Department, Infantry Field Manual, Rifle Company, Rifle Regiment, Chapter 6 Rifle Squad (1941), 134,

accessed December 20, 2014, http://www.ibiblio.org/hyperwar/ USA/ref/FM/FM7-10/FM7-10-6.html.

80. Dwight D. Eisenhower, *Crusade in Europe* (Garden City, NY: Doubleday 1948).

81. Letter from Donald H. Wedewer, 17 November 1944, Nancy and William Feld Papers. "Jerry" was a slang for Germans.

82. Letter from Donald H. Wedewer, 17 November 1944, Nancy and William Feld Papers.

## Chapter 7 Wounded

83. For a description of Viet's action for which he later received a Silver Star, see PFC James L. Haseltine ed., *From Battle Babies to Vets: The Combat History of the 394th Infantry Regiment*, n.p.

84. For a listing of lessons learned by the 394th Infantry Regiment during this period, see Headquarters 394th Infantry, "After Action Report (1–30 November 1944)."

85. Ibid.

86. The Catholic Tradition, *Traditional Catholic Prayers, Act of Contrition*, accessed February 8, 2015, http://www.catholictradition.org.

## Chapter 8 Surviving

87. U.S. Army Medical Department, Office of Medical History, Medical Department United States Army in World War II, Surgical Consultants to Field Armies in Theaters of Operation, Chapter XV Third U.S. Army, at 316, accessed February 8, 2015, http://history.amedd.army.mil/booksdocs/wwii/actvsurgconvoli/CH15.htm.

88. U.S. National Library of Medicine, National Institutes of

Health, Hypovolemic shock, accessed February 8, 2015, http://www.nlm.nih.gov/medlineplus/ency/article/000167.htm.

89. Ibid.

90. U.S. National Library of Medicine, National Institutes of Health, Amputation – traumatic, accessed February 8, 2015, http://www.nlm.nih.gov/medlineplus/ency/article/000006.htm.

91. Ibid.

92. U.S. National Library of Medicine, National Institutes of Health, Hypovolemic shock, accessed February 8, 2015, http://www.nlm.nih.gov/medlineplus/ency/article/000167.htm.

93. *ScienceDaily*, "Clotting Cells Switched on by Cold," accessed February 8, 2015, http://www.sciencedaily.com/releases/2002/03/020320081951.htm.

## Chapter 9 The City of Terror

94. Barbara W. Tuchman, *The Guns of August* (New York: Ballantine 1962), 164.

95. Ibid., 172.

96. Ibid., 166.

97. King and Kutta, *Impact: The History Of Germany's V-Weapons In World War II*, 283.

98. James Tobin, "Liege Under Siege," Medicine at Michigan 14, no. 2 (Summer 2012), accessed January 4, 2015, http://www.medicineatmichigan.org/sites/default/files/archives/lookingback_7.pdf. This article discusses the experience of the 298th General Hospital in Liège in 1944 during the V-1 attacks.

99. "Fayembois (Jupille) and the 16th General Hospital" (written by Second Lieutenant Muriel Phillips Engelman),

*Battle of The Bulge Memories*, last updated June 28, 2013, http://www.battleofthebulgememories.be/en/stories/us-army/365-fayembois-jupille-and-the-16th-general-hospital.html. "Fayembois (Jupille) and the 16th General Hospital (1st Lt Muriel Phillips Engelman, 16th General Hospital), Office de Promotion de Tourisme Wallonie-Bruxelles, accessed January 3, 2015, http://www.criba.be/fr/stories/detail/fayembois-jupille-and-the-16th-general-hospital-257-1. For a fuller account of Muriel Phillips Engelman's experience in Liège during the bombing, see Engelman, Murial P., *Mission Accomplished: Stop the Clock*, (Self-published, 2014).

100. King and Kutta, *Impact: The History of Germany's V-Weapons In World War II*, 285.

101. Ibid., 285.

102. Ibid., 283.

103. Ibid., 284.

104. For views of the hospital, see "Le domaine militaire Saint-Laurent," accessed January 4, 2015, http://www.cwarzee.net/3CRI/index.htm.

105. King and Kutta, *Impact: The History of Germany's V-Weapons In World War II*, introduction.

106. U.S. Army, 15th General Hospital, "Semi-Annual History, 15th General Hospital," 3.

107. Ibid., 285.

## Chapter 10 Heading Home

108. Letter from Donald H. Wedewer, Undated. Nancy and William Feld Papers.

109. "History DC-4/C-54 Skymaster Transport," Boeing Aircraft

Company, accessed January 2, 2015, http://www.boeing.com/boeing/history/mdc/dc-4.page.

110. A picture of Lajes Field in its World War II configuration can be found in: U.S. Air Force 65th Air Base Wing History Office, *A Short History of Lajes Field, Terceira Island, Azores, Portugal*, 3, accessed January 4, 2015, http://www.lajes.af.mil/shared/media/document/AFD-110621-022.pdf.

## Chapter 11 Stateside

111. "History C-47 Skytrain Military Transport," Boeing Aircraft Company, accessed January 2, 2015, http://www.boeing.com/boeing/history/mdc/skytrain.page.

## Chapter 12 Bushnell

112. Andrea Kay Carter, "Bushnell General Military Hospital and the Community of Brigham City, Utah During World War II" (master's thesis, Utah State University, 2008), 13. A further overview of the Bushnell hospital can be found in contemporary article about the hospital: Murray M. Moler, "Army Hospital in Brigham City Is City In Itself," *The Pittsburgh Press*, March 24, 1943.

113. Carter, "Bushnell General Military Hospital and the Community of Brigham City, Utah During World War II," 12.

114. Ibid., 10.

115. Ibid., 15.

116. Ibid., 13.

117. Ibid., 14.

118. Ibid.

119. Ibid., 52.

120. Ibid., 53.

## Chapter 13 To the West Coast

121. "Cut" Cunningham to Donald H. Wedewer, 7 May 1945. Donald H. Wedewer Papers, in the author's possession.

122. Ibid.

123. Ibid.

124. Ibid. For further information regarding Harrell C. Chambliss and Normal L. Venter, who are interned in the Netherlands, see "ABMC Burials and Memorializations," American Battle Monuments Commission, accessed January 5, 2015, https://www.abmc.gov/cemeteries-memorials#.V6IuAE1f1aS.

125. "Cut" Cunningham to Donald H. Wedewer, 7 May 1945. Donald H. Wedewer Papers, in the author's possession.

126. Ibid.

127. Ibid.

128. Decades later, Cut visited Dad in their one and only reunion after the war.

129. "Education Goal of Local Boy, Wedewer Who Lost Legs, Eye, Has Courage," *The Telegraph-Herald* (Dubuque, IA), July 22, 1945.

130. Ibid.

## Chapter 14 Walking

131. Carter, "Bushnell General Military Hospital and the Community of Brigham City, Utah During World War II," 19.

132. Ibid.

133. Ibid.

134. Ibid., 22.

135. Ibid., 23.

136. Carter, "Bushnell General Military Hospital and the Community of Brigham City, Utah During World War II," 59. To view additional information regarding the rehabilitation efforts of Joe Miller and the program at Bushnell, see "No Help Wanted," YouTube video, 17:23, posted by "Mr. Northview's channel," February 17, 2011, https://www.youtube.com/watch?v=TXUm0RuX-JI.

137. Carter, "Bushnell General Military Hospital and the Community of Brigham City, Utah During World War II," 59.

138. Maury Klein, *A Call To Arms: The Epic Story Of How America Mobilized For World War II* (New York: Bloomsbury 2013), 724.

139. Ibid.

140. Ibid.

141. Ibid., 40.

142. Ibid.

143. George Ford, "Both Legs Off, Yes; But Crippled? No!," *The Desert News* (Salt Lake City, UT), August 25, 1945.

144. "Strong Supporters of Forget-me-not Drive" *The Ogden Standard-Examiner* (Ogden, UT), November 23, 1945.

145. "History Silvestre Herrera," Herrera Elementary School (Phoenix, AZ), accessed December 28, 2014, http://phxschools.org/herrera/about/history/.

146. "Silvestre Herrera Obituary," Legacy.com, accessed December

28, 2014, http://www.legacy.com/obituaries/azcentral/obituary.aspx?n=silvestre-s-herrera&pid=98963690. This is a re-print of the obituary, see Silvestre S. Herrera Obituary, *The Arizona Republic*, December 2, 2007.

147. "Medal of Honor Silvestre S. Herrera," NBC News *The Daily Nightly* (July 23, 2007), accessed December 28, 2014, http://dailynightly.nbcnews.com/_news/2007/07/23/4372926-medal-of-honor-silvestre-s-herrera.

148. Ibid.

149. Ibid.

150. Dennis McLellan, "Silvestre Herrera 1916 – 2007," *Chicago Tribune*, December 3, 2007, http://articles.chicagotribune.com/2007-12-03/news/0712020276_1_silvestre-herrera-enemy-position-enemy-machine-gun.

151. To view the Herrera Medal of Honor citation, see "Medal of Honor Recipients, World War II (G-L)," Army Center on Military History, accessed January 4, 2015, http://www.history.army.mil/moh/wwII-g-l.html.

## Chapter 15 The Warrior

152. "Helen Keller Biography," American Foundation for the Blind, accessed December 28, 2014, http://www.afb.org/info/about-us/helen-keller/biography-and-chronology/biography/1235.

153. Helen Keller, *The Story of My Life* (Garden City, NY: Doubleday, 1914), 98.

154. "Helen Keller Biography," American Foundation for the Blind, accessed December 28, 2014, https://archive.org/details/storyofmylife00hele.

155. Blogpost Helen Keller's Words: 80 Years Later ... Still as

Powerful. Helen Selsdon, 5/9/2013. http://www.afb.org/blog/afb-blog/helen-kellers-words-80-years-later%e2%80%a6-still-as-powerful/12.

156. Ibid.

157. Sheryl Sandberg with Nell Scovell, *Lean In Women, Work, and the Will to Lead* (New York: Knopf, 2013).

158. Keller, *The Story of My Life*, 61.

## Chapter 16 Malcontent

159. "Battle Creek Sanitarium/Percy Jones Hospital," Michigan Historical Markers, accessed January 2, 2015, http://www.michmarkers.com/startup.asp?startpage=S0596.htm.

160. "Hart-Dole-Inouye Federal Center," U.S. General Services Administration, last reviewed November 11, 2013, http://www.gsa.gov/portal/content/102719.

## Chapter 17 Facing Reality

161. "A Brief History of Valley Forge General Hospital," Historical Society of the Phoenixville Area, accessed January 20, 2015, http://www.hspa-pa.org/History%20of%20Valley%20Forge%20Army%20Hospital.pdf.

162. *Bright Victory*, directed by Mark Robson (1951), DVD.

163. "Obstacle Perception," *Bright Victory*, directed by Mark Robson (1951), DVD.

164. Meyer Berger, "The Stirring Story of an American Town What Has Happened to Phoenixville, PA., Where Our Badly Wounded Learn to Live Again," *New York Times*, May 19, 1946.

165. Ibid.

166. Ibid.

167. Ibid.

## Chapter 18 Final Stop and Discharge

168. "A Brief History," Avon Old Farms School, accessed January 19, 2015, http://www.avonoldfarms.com/page.cfm?p=1237.

## Chapter 19 Mom

169. "Roosevelt Facts and Figures: The Great Depression," Franklin D. Roosevelt Presidential Library and Museum, accessed January 19, 2015, http://www.fdrlibrary.marist.edu.

170. "Cotton Club Fabled Speakeasy Where Duke Ellington First Won His Fame," Public Broadcasting System, accessed January 19, 2015, http://www.pbs.org/jazz/places/spaces_cotton_club.htm.

171. Ibid.

## Chapter 20 Off to College

172. The University Missouri Bulletin 47, no. 3, "For Veterans" (January. 20, 1946), University Archives-University of Missouri-Columbia.

173. Ibid., 35.

174. Ibid.

175. Winston Lord, "President's Corner," *The Missouri Student* (University of Missouri, Columbia, Missouri), December 17, 1947, University Archives, University of Missouri-Columbia.

176. Memorandum to the [University] President, "On Organization Required for Discipline Cases," November 29, 1949, University Archives, University of Missouri-Columbia.

177. Enrollment History of University of Missouri Beginning 1842 (Fall Headcount) University Archives, University of Missouri-Columbia.

178. Robert M. Gates: "Lecture at Duke University (All-Volunteer Force)." September, 29, 2010. http://www.defense.gov/speeches.

## Chapter 21 Engagement, Marriage and Graduation

179. "Commencement, June, 1950 Menu served at President Middlebrush's luncheon for President Truman," University Archives, University of Missouri-Columbia.

180. "President Truman Joins Sister In an Impromptu Piano Duet Event for Fifty Guests in Home of M. U. President Is Followed by Excerpts From Some of the Classical Selections," *Kansas City Star*, June 10, 1050, University Archives, University of Missouri-Columbia.

181. David McCullough, *Truman* (New York: Simon & Schuster, 1992), 955.

182. "Executive Order 9981," Harry S. Truman Library & Museum, accessed November 22, 2015, http://www.trumanlibrary.org/executiveorders/index.php?pid=869&st=9981&st1=.

183. McCullough, *Truman*, 613-618.

184. Joseph Driscoll, "Truman Make Phi Beta Kappa Hard Way: Didn't Go to College Father's Financial Reverses Caused Him to Go to Work After High School – He Studied Law, but Never Finished," St. Louis Post-Dispatch, June 10, 1950, University Archives, University of Missouri-Columbia.

185. Ibid.

186. Ibid.

187. "Truman Leaves Washington Today for Speech at M.U.; Fair Weather in Prospect Showers Will End By Dawn City and University Complete Plans for Truman Visit," *Columbia Daily Tribune* (Columbia, MO), June 8, 1950, University Archives, University of Missouri-Columbia.

188. Ibid.

189. "1752 Get Degrees, Set M.U. Record 3 Emeritus Titles Presented Today To Faculty Members," *Columbia Daily Tribune* (Columbia, MO), June 9, 1950, University Archives, University of Missouri-Columbia.

190. Ibid.

191. Degrees Awarded June 1950, University of Missouri, Office of Public Information, University Archives, University of Missouri-Columbia.

192. "Truman at Columbia," *St. Louis Globe Democrat*, June 10, 1950, University Archives, University of Missouri-Columbia.

193. "Public Papers of the Presidents Harry S. Truman 1945-1953 Commencement Address at the University of Missouri June 9, 1950," Harry S. Truman Library & Museum, accessed January 10, 2015, http://www.trumanlibrary.org/publicpapers/index.php?pid=786&st=&st1=.

194. Ibid.

195. Ibid.

## Chapter 22 South Florida and Next Steps

196. Studs Terkel, *The Good War: An Oral History of World War II* (New York: Pantheon 1985).

## Chapter 23 Sears and Hitting Bottom

197. "Sputnik and The Dawn of the Space Age," National Aeronautics and Space Administration, accessed January 23, 2015, http://history.nasa.gov/sputnik/.

## Chapter 24 The Call to Public Service

198. United States Blind Golf Association, accessed January 17, 2015, http://www.blindgolf.com.

199. "Hall of Fame Inductees," United States Blind Golf Association, http://www.usblindgolf.com/usbga-bob-andrews.pdf.

200. American Foundation for the Blind website, Helen Keller quotations page, http://www.afb.org/info/about-us/helen-keller/quotes/125.

201. Donald D. Foos and Nancy C. Pack, *History of the Florida Division Blind Services First Fifty Years* (1941–1991) (Florida Division of Blind Services Bureau of Library Services for the Blind and Physically Handicapped1992), 80-85.

202. Ibid., 85

203. Ibid.

204. Memorandum by Donald H. Wedewer, The Donald H. Wedewer Era as Director of the Division of Blind Services, Donald H. Wedewer Papers, in the author's possession.

205. The President's Committee on Employment of the Handicapped, *Performance* (February 1970), 2.

206. Claude R. Kirk, Jr. to Donald H. Wedewer, January 27, 1970, Donald H. Wedewer Papers, in the author's possession.

207. "Blind Amputee Is Honored as Worker of Year," *Miami Herald* (April 1970).

208. Helen Keller Speech in Washington, D.C. 1925, available on the American Foundation for the Blind website, http://www.afb.org/info/about-us/helen-keller/letters/franklin-d-roosevelt/address-in-washington-dc-1925/12345.

209. Charles B. MacDonald, *A Time For Trumpets: The Untold Story Of The Battle Of The Bulge* (New York: Quill William Morrow, 1985).

## Chapter 25 The Pinnacle

210. *Foos and Pack, History of the Florida Division Blind Services First Fifty Years* (1941–1991), 1.

211. Ibid., 2.

212. Ibid., 21.

213. Helen Keller to Spessard Holland, 28 May 1941. Helen Keller Archives, American Foundation for the Blind.

214. John F. Kennedy, "The President's News Conference," April 21, 1961. Online by Gerhard Peters and John T. Woolley, The American Presidency Project, University of California Santa Barbara, http://www.presidency.ucsb.edu/ws/?pid=8077.

215. Ronald Reagan, letter to Donald H. Wedewer, November 10, 1987, Donald H. Wedewer Papers, in the author's possession.

216. S.R. 1310 A resolution relating to Days of Remembrance of the Victims of the Holocaust, Journal of the Florida Senate, No. 14, 232 (May 7, 1985), http://archive.flsenate.gov/data/Historical/Senate%20Journals/1980s/1985/26-218TO23405_07_85.PDF.

217. Journal of the Florida Senate, No. 14, 232 (May 7, 1985), http://archive.flsenate.gov/data/Historical/Senate%20

Journals/1980s/1985/26-218TO23405_07_85.PDF (A photo of the event can be found at https://www.floridamemory.com).

218. Nomination for Florida Association of Rehabilitation Secretaries Boss of the Year Award 1974, Donald H. Wedewer Papers, in the author's possession.

219. Foos and Pack, *History of the Florida Division Blind Services First Fifty Years* (1941–1991), 76.

220. Ibid.

221. Ibid., 77.

222. Memorandum by Donald H. Wedewer, The Donald H. Wedewer Era as Director of the Division of Blind Services, Donald H. Wedewer Papers, in the author's possession.

223. Ibid.

224. Ibid.

225. So long, Don! We'll miss you!, June 5, 1989, Donald H. Wedewer Papers, in the author's possession.

226. "AFB Migel Medal Awards," American Foundation for the Blind, accessed January 17, 2015, http://www.afb.org/info/about-us/events-and-awards/migel-medal-awards/123.

227. "About Us More Than 90 Years of Advocacy and Support for People with Vision Loss," American Foundation for the Blind, accessed January 17, 2015, http://www.afb.org/info/about-us/history/12.

228. "Previous Migel Medal Honorees," American Foundation for the Blind, accessed January 17, 2015, http://www.afb.org/info/about-us/events-and-awards/migel-medal-awards/previous-honorees/1235.

229. *1990 Migel Medal Award For Distinguished Achievement on*

*Behalf of Blind and Visually Impaired People.* New York: American Foundation for the Blind, 1990. Event program.

230. George H.W. Bush and Barbara Bush to Donald H. Wedewer and Abram Claude, Jr., October 15, 1990, Donald H. Wedewer Papers, in the author's possession.

## Chapter 26 Final Calling

231. The White House, Office of the Press Secretary, "President Clinton Appoints Four Members to the Committee for Purchase From People Who Are Blind or Severely Disabled," press release, April 13, 1994, http://clinton6.nara.gov/1994/04/1994-04-13-appointments-to-committee-for-purchases-from-disabled.html.

232. Ibid.

233. Ibid.

234. Ibid.

235. Lisa Bacot, Executive Director, Commission for the Transportation Disadvantaged, "Overview of the Florida Transportation Disadvantaged Program" (presentation, Regional Transportation Summit – Building a Path to Regional Partnerships Lake-Sumter Metropolitan Planning Organization, October 27, 2005).

236. Center for Urban Transportation Research, University of South Florida, Tampa, *1998 Florida Transportation Almanac*, Table 3-37, 139 (this document cites as a source the Florida Commission for the Transportation Disadvantaged, 1997 Annual Performance Report (January 1998)).

237. Bob Norman, "Capitol Offenses, The trial of former Florida House Speaker Bo Johnson reveals the unseemly roles of Broward's taxi mogul Jesse Gaddis and lobbyist Tom Panza," *Broward Palm Beach New Times News*, May 13, 1999, http://www.browardpalmbeach.com.

# SELECTED BIBLIOGRAPHY

*Bright Victory*. Directed by Mark Robson. Universal International Pictures, 1951. DVD.

Carter, Andrea Kay. "Bushnell General Military Hospital and the Community of Brigham City, Utah During World War II." Masters thesis, Utah State University, 2008.

Chang, Iris. *The Rape of Nanking*. New York: Basic Books 2011.

*Dyersville, Iowa Centennial July 9 –15, 1972*. Published by the Dyersville Area Centennial Corporation. Official History & Program.

Eisenhower, Dwight D. *Crusade in Europe*. Garden City, NY: Doubleday, 1948.

Engelman, Murial P. "Interview U.S. Army Nurse at Battle of the Bulge" – WWII.mov. https:/www.youtube.com/.

Engelman, Murial P. *Mission Accomplished: Stop the Clock*. Self-published, 2014.

Feld, Nancy and William Papers. Copies provided to the author.

*Field of Dreams*, Anniversary Edition DVD. Directed by Phil Alden Robinson. Universal City, CA: 2004.

Foos, Donald D. and Nancy C. Park. *History of the Florida Division of Blind Services: First 50 Years (1941 – 1991)*. Photocopy, Bureau of Braille and Talking Book Library Services, Daytona Beach, Florida.

Gibran, Daniel K. *"The 92nd Infantry Division and the Italian Campaign in World War II."* Jefferson, NC: McFarland, 2001.

Haseltine, PFC James L., ed. *From Battle Babies to Vets: The Combat History of the 394th Infantry Regiment.* Photocopy, National Archives and Records Administration, College Park, Maryland.

Headquarters 394th Infantry. "After Action Report (1–30 November 1944)." Photocopy, National Archives and Records Administration, College Park, Maryland.

Headquarters 394th Infantry. "History of the 394th Infantry Regiment, 99th Infantry Division, 1 January 1944 through 31 December 1944." Photocopy, National Archives and Records Administration, College Park, Maryland.

Heller, Joseph. *Catch-22.* New York: Simon & Schuster, 1961. Reprinted with a new introduction by Christopher Buckley. New York: Simon & Schuster, 2011.

Herodatus. *The Histories.* Digireads.com Publishing, 2009.

Jenkins, Sam. "The Digital Collections of the National World War II Museum." Segment 2. http://ww2online.org/.

Keller, Helen. *The Story of My Life.* Garden City, NY: Doubleday, 1914. https://archive.org/.

Keller, Helen. *We Bereaved.* New York: Leslie Fulenwider, 1929. https://archive.org/.

King, Benjamin and Timothy J. Kutta. *Impact: The History of Germany's V-Weapons in World War II,* New York: Sarpedon, 1998.

Klein, Maury. *A Call To Arms: The Epic Story Of How America Mobilized For World War* II. New York: Bloomsbury 2013.

MacDonald, Charles B. *A Time For Trumpets: The Untold Story Of The Battle Of The Bulge.* New York: Quill William Morrow, 1985.

McCullough, David. *Truman.* New York: Simon & Schuster, 1992.

McLean, Douglas M. "The Battle of Convoy BX-141." *Northern Mariner* 3, no. 4 (1993): 19-35. Accessed January 3, 2015. http://www.cnrs-scrn.org/.

Mortensen, Dan. *You Would Have To Be Blind Not To See It ...* February 9, 2009. Valley Forge, Pennsylvania: 2009. DVD.

National Association of Mutual Insurance Companies. "No Help Wanted." 1945. 17:23. YouTube video posted by Mr. Northview, February 17, 2011. https://www.youtube.com/.

Office of Strategic Services Research and Analysis Branch. *Current Intelligence Study Number 35*. http://www.foia.cia.gov/.

Office of the Theater Historian, European Theater of Operations. *Order of Battle of the United States Army World War II, European Theater of Operations*. December 1945. http://www.history.army.mil/.

Sandberg, Sheryl with Nell Scovell. *Lean In Women, Work, and the Will to Lead*. New York: Knopf, 2013.

Schlarman, Vicki, ed. *The Wedewer Family Reunion Book 1994*. Dubuque, Iowa.

Selsdon, Helen. *Helen Keller's Words: 80 Years Later ... Still as Powerful* (blog). http://www.afb.org/.

Terkel, Studs. *The Good War: An Oral History of World War II*. New York: Pantheon, 1985.

Tobin, James. "Liege Under Siege." *Medicine at Michigan* 14, no. 2 (Summer 2012). http://www.medicineatmichigan.org/.

Tuchman, Barbara W. *The Guns of August*. New York: Ballantine, 1962.

Unit Journal 394th Infantry. Photocopy, National Archives and Records Administration, College Park, Maryland.

U.S. Army. *Camp Wolters Infantry Replacement Training Center Guide.* Mineral Wells, Texas. http://www.fortwolters.com/.

U.S. Army, 15th General Hospital. "Semi-Annual History 15th General Hospital, 1 January 1945 – 30 June 1945."

U.S. Army Historical Section. *Army Ground Forces Study No. 7 Provision of Enlisted Replacements, Functional of the Replacement System in 1942.* http://www.history.army.mil/.

U.S. Army, Infantry Replacement Training Center, *IRTC I am a Doughboy.* http://www.fortwolters.com/.

U.S. Army Medical Department, Office of Medical History. "Official History Medical Department of the United States Army in World War II, Cold Injury, Ground Type." http://history.amedd.army.mil/.

U.S. Army Medical Department, Office of Medical History. "Medical Department United States Army in World War II, Surgical Consultants to Field Armies in Theaters of Operation, Chapter XV Third U.S. Army." http://history.amedd.army.mil/.

U.S. Army Service Forces Signal Corps. "Rifle U.S. Cal. .30 M1." War Department Training Film T.F.9 1172. 1943. YouTube video posted by Arms Control Center on July 29, 2010. https://www.youtube.com/.

U.S. Army Signal Corps. "Kill or Be Killed." War Department Training Film, T.F. 21 1024. 1943. YouTube video posted by Jeff Quitney on February 26, 2012. https://www.youtube.com/.

U.S. Government, War Department. "Infantry Field Manual, Rifle Company, Rifle Regiment, Chapter 6 Rifle Squad" (1941). http://www.ibiblio.org/.

Wedewer, Donald H. Papers. In the author's possession.

Wedewer, Marabeth S. Papers. In the author's possession.

# ABOUT THE AUTHOR

Harry Wedewer is a retired U.S. Navy Commander. On active duty he served as a Naval Flight Officer and Aerospace Engineering Duty Officer. He currently is a practicing attorney in public service. Harry is a 1983 graduate of The Citadel, The Military College of South Carolina and received his J.D. from the Georgetown University Law Center in Washington, D.C. in 2004. He is a prior contributor to the U.S. Naval Institute *Proceedings*. Harry resides in Southern Maryland with his wife Robin.

Made in the USA
Monee, IL
21 October 2024